CHAPTER 1

My Noble Son, I must tell you an ancient tale—a dark tale of monsters and magic, villains and heroes, with names you do not know, but whose story echoes even today...

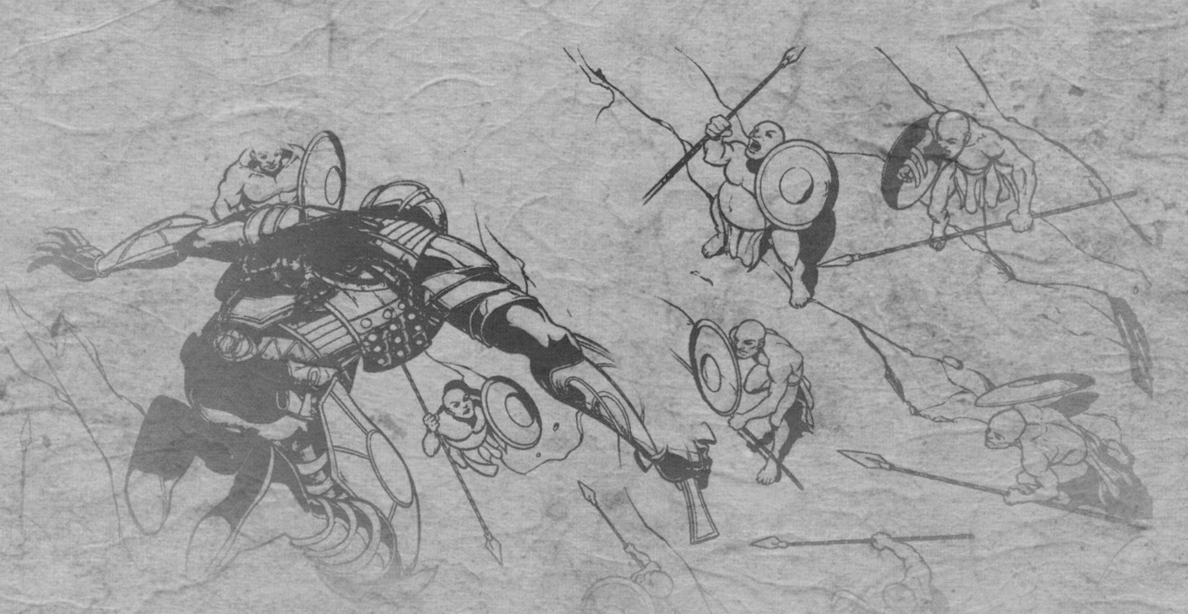

COMMUNITY OUTREACH CENTER, TONIGHT

YAAAH! AHH ARGH!
WHAT IS ALL THAT NOISE? WHAT'S GOING ON OUT THERE?
ANGER
EXPLOSIVE

BAMF

WHAT ARE YOU SUPPOSED TO BE?

WE MET THE OTHER NIGHT AT THE WHARF.

SKI MASK? THE HELMET IS AN UPGRADE. SORRY ABOUT THE OLD LADY.

CHK
CHK
NO YOU'RE NOT AND IT MAKES WHAT I'M ABOUT TO DO ALL THE MORE SATISFYING.

YOU *REALLY* THINK YOU CAN TAKE *ALL TWENTY OF US* ON YOUR OWN?

I REALIZE IT'S NOT A FAIR FIGHT...

BADDA
BADDA

SLRSH
BLAM
BLAM

KRAAASH
BLAM
BLAM
BLAM
BLAM
SLRSH
SLRSH

TNK
TNK
TNK
TNK

BLAM
BLAM
BRAKKA
BRAKKA
BRAKKA

HYUNH!

RAHH!

tnk
THOK

AAHH!

KLUNK

...FOR YOU.

WHAP

THIS IS FOR --

WAKOOOM

BOOOOOM

THWAK

KRUNCH
OOF!

LEGEND OF THE MANTAMAJI™

CREATED AND WRITTEN BY
ERIC DEAN SEATON

ART BY
BRANDON PALAS

COLORS BY
ANDREW DALHOUSE

LETTERS BY
DERON BENNETT

EDITED BY
DAVID ELLIS DICKERSON

10061 Riverside Drive, Suite 296 Toluca Lake, California 91602. Published by "And... Action!" Entertainment © ™ All Eyes On E, Inc. Printed in Korea. ISBN 978-1-930315-34-1

MANHATTAN, NEW YORK
THREE DAYS AGO
THIS IS SADIE WEST, LIVE FROM THE JUSTICE CENTER WHERE ASSISTANT DISTRICT ATTORNEY ELIJAH ALEXANDER, STILL FILLING IN FOR AILING D.A. CHRIS PHILLIPS, HAS JUST WON A GUN TRAFFICKING CONVICTION FOR ORGANIZED CRIME BOSS MICHAEL HARRISON.

CONGRATULATIONS, MR. ALEXANDER. THE JURY RETURNED THEIR VERDICT IN JUST FIVE HOURS. WHAT DO YOU THINK THAT MEANS?

IT MEANS THAT THE DEFENSE WAS GOOD, BUT I WAS BETTER AND THE JURY WAS SMART.
IN FACT, I'VE REQUESTED THE SAME JURY FOR ALL MY TRIALS!

NEW WORLD KNIGHTS! THAT'S WHAT THEY CALL THEMSELVES!
THEY SET ME UP! I SWEAR! NOBODY'S SAFE. NOBODY!
THIS IS THE SIXTH STRAIGHT CASE IN WHICH THE DEFENSE CLAIMED THEIR CLIENTS WERE SET UP.

THERE'S NO EVIDENCE THAT A MYSTERIOUS STREET GANG IS CONTROLLING ALL THE CRIME IN THE EAST. WE'VE INVESTIGATED. THE NEW WORLD KNIGHTS ARE A MYTH. KIND OF A WEIRD ONE, FRANKLY.
THEN WHY DO YOU THINK THAT DEFENSE KEEPS COMING UP?

BECAUSE MR. HARRISON'S ATTORNEYS KNOW THAT THE PUBLIC LOVES A GOOD CONSPIRACY THEORY.
IT'S DUMB, BUT TRUE.

PARANOIA? GROUPTHINK? PEOPLE LOVE TO RUMINATE ON THE *"HIDDEN WORLD"* THAT EXISTS BEHIND OUR OWN.

BARNUM SAID YOU COULD NEVER GO BROKE UNDERESTIMATING THE INTELLIGENCE OF THE PUBLIC. APPARENTLY, THAT WAS THE MOTTO OF MY HIGH-PRICED OPPONENTS' LAW SCHOOLS.

LADIES AND GENTLEMEN, I THINK AT THIS POINT ANY FURTHER QUESTIONS SHOULD BE ADDRESSED TO THE DEFENSE. THANK YOU.

THAT'S THE FIRST TIME YOU'VE *EVER* CUT AN INTERVIEW SHORT. YOU GET STRUCK BY A BOLT OF HUMILITY?
NO, I GOT MY EYE ON A *BIGGER* PRIZE.

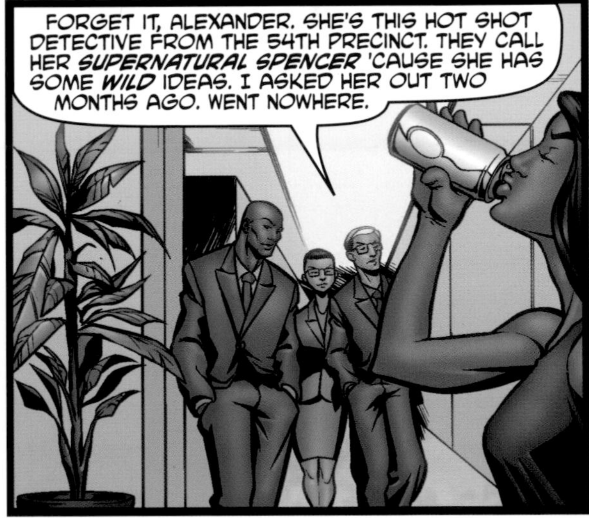
FORGET IT, ALEXANDER. SHE'S THIS HOT SHOT DETECTIVE FROM THE 54TH PRECINCT. THEY CALL HER *SUPERNATURAL SPENCER* 'CAUSE SHE HAS SOME *WILD* IDEAS. I ASKED HER OUT TWO MONTHS AGO. WENT NOWHERE.

REALLY? WELL, TAKE NOTES. EVERY WORD OUT OF MY MOUTH IS MAGIC.
LUNCH SAYS I'LL BOOK HER BEFORE THE ELEVATOR COMES.
I'LL TAKE THAT BET.

EXCUSE ME. I JUST WANTED TO ASK IF YOU'RE AS UPSET AS I AM?
ABOUT WHAT?
WELL, WE BOTH WORK IN CITY GOVERNMENT, WE MUST HAVE AT LEAST ONE MUTUAL FRIEND.
AND WHY SHOULD I BE UPSET IF WE DO?

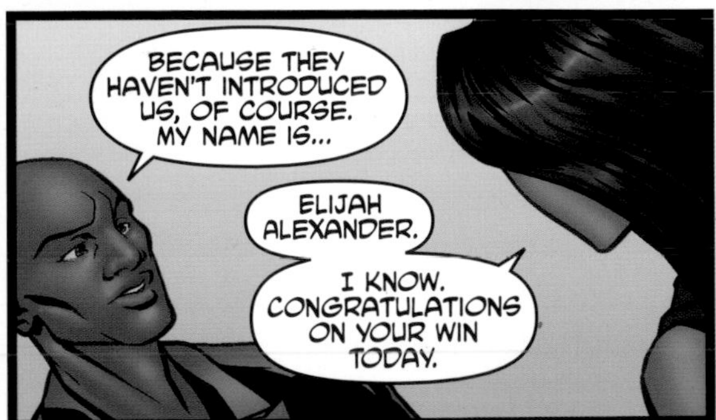
BECAUSE THEY HAVEN'T INTRODUCED US, OF COURSE. MY NAME IS...
ELIJAH ALEXANDER.
I KNOW. CONGRATULATIONS ON YOUR WIN TODAY.

JUST ANOTHER DAY AT THE OFFICE.
SO, UM, DETECTIVE SPENCER...
SYDNEY.
CAN HE BE ANY MORE SMUG?
I FIND IT SEXY.

SYDNEY, IS THERE SOME SORT OF REWARD FOR HELPING TO KEEP THE STREETS CLEAN?

WHAT KIND OF REWARD ARE YOU LOOKING FOR, COUNSELOR?

I DON'T KNOW. I WAS HOPING TO GET "THE GIRL."

SOUNDS INTRIGUING, ALTHOUGH YOU'RE IGNORING ONE IMPORTANT DETAIL.
DING
AND WHAT WOULD THAT BE?

"THE GIRL" ISN'T A TROPHY YOU CAN WIN.
SHADE.

WE'LL BRING YOU THE RECEIPT, ELIJAH.

FUNNY, VERY FUNNY. HOW ARE YOU GONNA PLAY ME LIKE THAT?
I LIKE YOU, ELIJAH, BUT NOT EVERYTHING CAN BE ALL ABOUT YOU.

IT'S NOT. I WAS JUST TRYING TO SHOW I HAVE MY EYES ON MORE THAN JUST WINNING ANOTHER CASE.
YEAH, LIKE WHAT?
YOU.

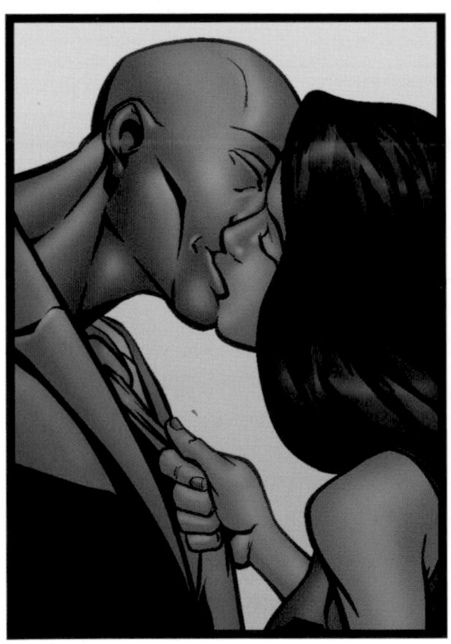

THERE'S MY KISS.

YOU'RE SO FULL OF IT.
JURY DIDN'T THINK SO.

DON'T YOU FEEL THESE CASES ARE *TOO* EASY?

HERE WE GO AGAIN.
I'M JUST SAYING. IN THE PAST SIX MONTHS ONE SYNDICATE AFTER ANOTHER HAS FALLEN LIKE--

DOMINOS.
WE'VE BEEN DOWN THIS ROAD.

EVERYTHING IS HAPPENING BECAUSE OF HARD WORK BY THE N.Y.P.D. AND THE D.A.'S OFFICE, NOT SOME STREET GANG THAT DOESN'T LEAVE A PHYSICAL OR ELECTRONIC TRACE.
I GUESS I'M JUST A SKEPTIC.
WELL, HAVE MORE FAITH. IF NOT IN YOUR CO-WORKERS, THEN IN ME.

SO, I'LL SEE YOU TONIGHT FOR A LATE DINNER?
ABSOLUTELY.

AND YOU'RE GOING TO WEAR THAT DRESS I BOUGHT YOU?

ABSOLUTELY *NOT.* IT MAKES ME LOOK LIKE AN EIGHTY-YEAR-OLD NUN.

SYD, MY MOM IS VERY TRADITIONAL. I WANT THIS TO GET OFF ON THE RIGHT FOOT.
OKAY, THEN GIVE THE DRESS TO *HER* TO WEAR... *SIGH* C'MON, WILL IT MAKE A DIFFERENCE?
NYPD

WE ATE RICE AND BEANS FOR TWO YEARS SO I COULD GET MY ASSOCIATE'S DEGREE. STRIVING TO HAVE THE BEST IS BASED OFF WHAT I LEARNED FROM HER.
YOU ARE THE FIRST WOMAN I'VE EVER WANTED TO INTRODUCE HER TO. I JUST WANT TO DO IT RIGHT.
I HAVE TO ADMIT, IT INTRIGUES ME THAT A MAN SO CONFIDENT CARES SO MUCH ABOUT WHAT HIS MOTHER THINKS.
AND...
I'LL SEE YOU TONIGHT.
AND...
AND...I'LL WEAR THE DRESS.
YOU WON'T REGRET IT.

GRAND CENTRAL STATION

The New York Times

District Attorney Elijah Alexander Does It Again

EXCUSE ME.

HERE YOU GO.

LET ME LOOK AT YOU. PEANUT, YOU'RE STILL SKINNY.
BEEN WORKING OUT. KICK BOXING NOW.

WHAT'S WITH THIS OLD BAG? DID YOU GET THE MONEY I SENT YOU?
I ALWAYS DO, BUT THE MALL WAS CLOSED IN THE REMOTE *BRAZILIAN* RAIN FOREST WHERE I WAS WORKING.

POINT TAKEN.
BY THE WAY, I'VE BEEN WORKING TOO.
District Attorne
Alexander Does
ARE YOU IN *EVERY* PAPER?

PAPER, TV, YOU NAME IT. YOUR BOY IS BIG TIME.
THE CONTACTS AND PRESS I'M GETTING FROM THESE HIGH PROFILE CASES IS GOING TO ALLOW ME TO WALK RIGHT OUT OF THE D.A.'S OFFICE INTO A PARTNERSHIP AT ONE OF THE BIGGEST PRACTICES IN THE CITY.
BUT WILL THAT ALLOW YOU TO MAKE THIS WORLD A *BETTER* PLACE?
THE TRUE TEST OF A MAN'S CONSCIENCE IS HIS WILLINGNESS TO SACRIFICE.

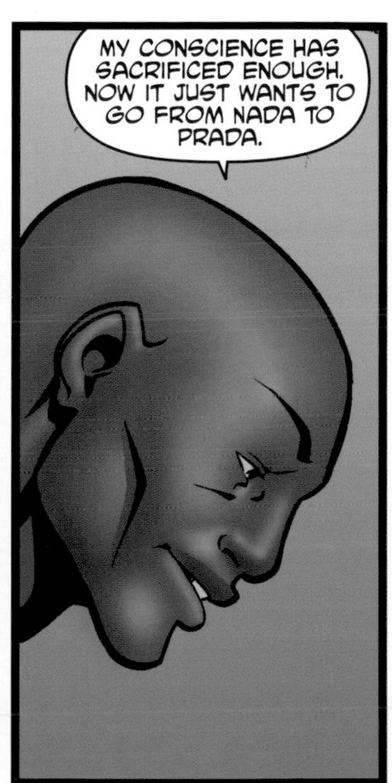
MY CONSCIENCE HAS SACRIFICED ENOUGH. NOW IT JUST WANTS TO GO FROM NADA TO PRADA.

WHEN YOU GO THROUGH HARDSHIP AND DECIDE NOT TO SURRENDER. THAT IS *BROTHER HOPE.*
ONLY A FOOL TRIPS OVER HIS PAST. BROTHER HOPE IS THE WAY.
WHAT'S YOUR BIGGEST FEAR? BROTHER HOPE IS BIGGER.
BROTHER HOPE
DO YOU NEED A COT? WE'VE GOT A PLACE. STAY AS LONG AS YOU WANT TO LEARN.

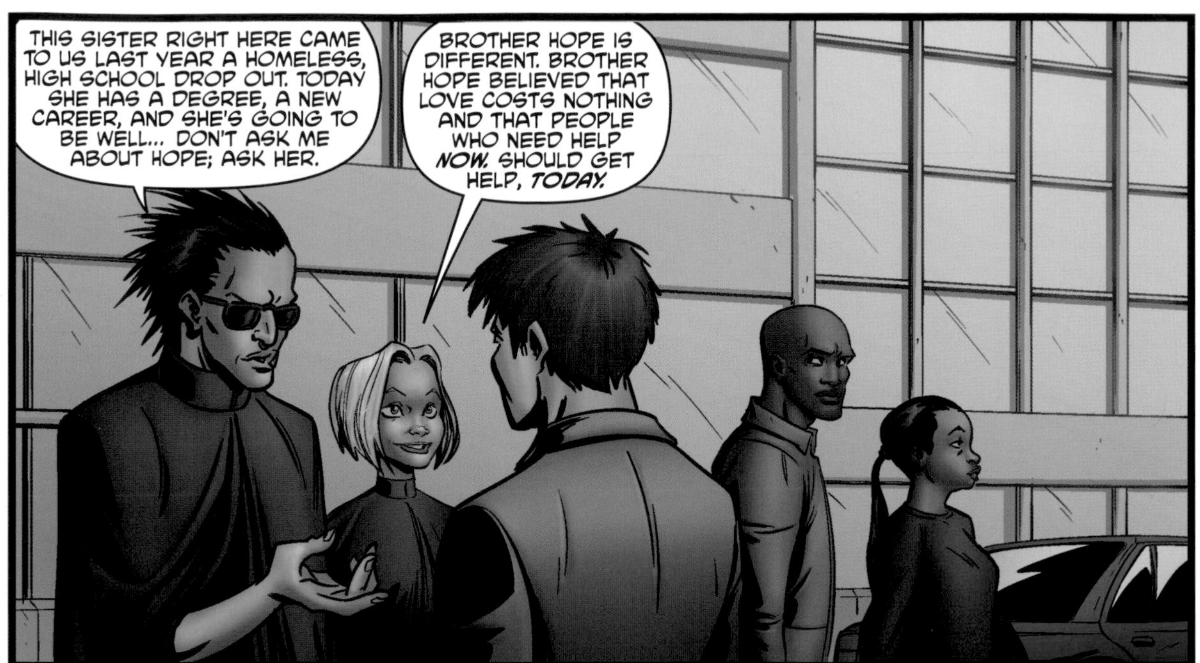
THIS SISTER RIGHT HERE CAME TO US LAST YEAR A HOMELESS, HIGH SCHOOL DROP OUT. TODAY SHE HAS A DEGREE, A NEW CAREER, AND SHE'S GOING TO BE WELL... DON'T ASK ME ABOUT HOPE; ASK HER.
BROTHER HOPE IS DIFFERENT. BROTHER HOPE BELIEVED THAT LOVE COSTS NOTHING AND THAT PEOPLE WHO NEED HELP *NOW.* SHOULD GET HELP, *TODAY.*

NAMASTE, SISTER.
ONCE YOU CHOOSE HOPE, ANYTHING'S POSSIBLE.

WHO IS BROTHER HOPE?
HE'S THIS NEW AGE EMPOWERMENT PREACHER WHO'S BIG HERE ON THE EAST COAST.
YOU'D LIKE HIM MOM, 'CAUSE LIKE YOUR SON, HE'S TRYING TO BE THE FACE OF THE FUTURE.

BROTHER HOPE

ADL-46

EXCUSE ME, SIR. YOU DON'T HAVE TO REMAIN HOMELESS.

-!-

IF YOU CALL OUT FOR HELP, I WILL END YOU BEFORE THEY CAN PROTECT YOU.
KELLIS, WE'RE LEAVING.

COME ON, LET'S GO.

PICK UP THE PAPERS.

GO.
BROTHER HOPE

WHEN WE CALL, YOU HAVE YOU HAVE TO WRAP IT UP, KELLIS. OUR LORD CALLED. IT'S TIME TO GO TO WORK.

HARLEM, NEW YORK.

THIS PLACE COULD USE A WOMAN'S TOUCH. WHILE YOU'RE FLYING FIRST CLASS, YOUR FURNITURE IS STUCK IN COACH.

IT STILL BEATS THAT ONE BEDROOM WE HAD IN NORTH DAKOTA.

HELLO.
HEY. COME ON IN.
MOM, THIS IS SYDNEY.
IT'S A PLEASURE TO MEET YOU.
SO THIS IS THE WOMAN MY SON HAS BEEN GOING ON AND ON ABOUT FOR THE PAST NINE MONTHS?
HE SAID YOU WERE BEAUTIFUL, BUT HE DIDN'T DO YOU JUSTICE.
WELL, THANK YOU, MS. ALEXANDER. ON AND ON, HUH?
SHE WAS HALFWAY AROUND THE WORLD IN A RAINFOREST. WE HAD TO HAVE *SOMETHING* TO TALK ABOUT.

WHAT DO YOU HAVE THERE?
MY MOTHER'S BOOK OF LEGENDS.
WE WERE SO POOR, SHE WOULD CREATE THESE STORIES AS A WAY FOR US TO PLAY.

EVERY STORY HAD A *PURPOSE.* I WANTED PEANUT TO UNDERSTAND ABOUT RESPONSIBILITIES AND CHOICES.
PEANUT?
YOU DIDN'T HEAR THAT.
THAT'S AMAZING. YOU MUST HAVE A VERY CREATIVE MIND.

OH, THEY ARE GRAND EPIC ADVENTURES SPANNING THOUSANDS OF YEARS. VERY "LORD OF THE RINGS."
DID YOU EVER THINK OF PUBLISHING THEM?
NO, THEY WERE JUST FOR ME AND MY SON.

I THINK THAT'S GREAT. I WOULD HAVE *LOVED* TO HAVE A MOTHER WHO COULD HAVE TOLD ME SUCH INCREDIBLE STORIES.

MAYBE YOU CAN TELL THEM TO MY GRANDCHILDREN ONE DAY.
BEEP♪ ♪BEEP

SAVED BY THE *CELL.*

HELLO.
OKAY, I'M ON MY WAY.

I'M SORRY, BUT I HAVE TO LEAVE.
YOU *JUST* GOT HERE.

I KNOW. I'M SO SORRY. BUT I'VE BEEN WORKING ON A BIG CASE AND I THINK I GOT THE LEAD I'VE BEEN WAITING FOR.
I'LL MAKE THIS UP TO YOU BOTH.

IT WAS NICE MEETING YOU.
THANK YOU, MS. ALEXANDER.

YOU FORGOT A LITTLE SOMETHING...
DON'T TRY IT.
BYE, PEANUT.

I KNOW IT WAS BRIEF BUT WHAT DO YOU THINK?

SEEMS NICE. AND, HER ANTIQUE STYLE OF DRESS FITS RIGHT IN WITH YOUR FURNITURE.

THE MUSEUM OF NATURAL HISTORY

DETECTIVE SPENCER, N.Y.P.D. OPEN UP! I NEED TO SPEAK TO YOUR HEAD OF SECURITY.

WHAT'S THE PROBLEM?

WEEOOO
WEE EOOOO

WEEEOOOOOOO
WEEEOOOO

FACE DOWN ON THE FLOOR, NOW!

BRAKKA
BRAKKA

BLAM
BLAM

BLAM
BLAM
BLAM

SWOOSH

BRRAKK BRRAKKK

BLAM
BRAKKA BLAM
BRAKKA

BRRAKK
BLAM
BLAM

FALL BACK! NOW!

BLAM
BLAM
BLAM
BLAM
BRAKKA
BLAM
BRAKKA
BRAKKA
BLAM
BLAM

BLAM
BLAM
BLAM

GO!
GO!
MY LORD, WE NEED YOUR HELP!

WHERE DID THEY GO? WHICH WAY?

TO BE CONTINUED

CHAPTER 2

They were everyday people-fishwives and farmers, old peasants and young princes—the children of the chosen. They were willing to make great sacrifices to keep our world safe. Sometimes they lost everything. They did not count the cost.

MUSEUM OF NATURAL HISTORY,
THREE NIGHTS AGO.
COMMANDER COTTON, FIFTH PRECINCT.
I NEED A LIST OF EVERY ARTIFACT PUT ON DISPLAY WITHIN THE LAST WEEK.
WHERE IT CAME FROM, WHO DISCOVERED IT. *EVERYTHING.*

SPENCER! TEN SECURITY GUARDS WOUNDED, FOUR IN CRITICAL CONDITION, PRICELESS ARTIFACTS RIDDLED WITH BULLET HOLES. WHAT HAPPENED HERE?
IT WAS THE NEW WORLD KNIGHTS.

I DIDN'T KNOW WE OFFICIALLY PROVED THEY EXISTED! HOW DID THEY GET IN THE BUILDING WITHOUT TIPPING THE ALARMS?
I BELIEVE THEY WERE HERE WHEN THE MUSEUM CLOSED.

HIDING WHERE?
I'M NOT SURE.
AND THEN THEY JUST SAID WHAT THE HELL AND SMASHED AND GRABBED ONLY ONE ARTIFACT? ARE THEY SUBTLE OR NOT?
I KNOW IT'S NOT TRACKING YET, SIR.

THEN YOU SEE WHERE I'M GOING HERE, SPENCER?

I SAW THEM, SIR.
WHAT DID THEY LOOK LIKE?
THEY WORE MASKS.
WITH THE NAME "NEW WORLD KNIGHTS" ON THE FRONT?
I KNOW THIS LOOKS BAD.
BAD? BAD WOULD BE A VAST IMPROVEMENT OVER THIS CATASTROPHE! YOU KNOW WHAT THEY CALL YOU, SPENCER?

DON'T REALLY CARE, SIR.
WELL, YOU SHOULD.

EVERYONE TOLD ME YOU WERE THIS BRIGHT, SMART, GROUNDED COP. OVER THE PAST FEW MONTHS I'VE SEEN *NONE* OF THAT. I RUN A TIGHT SHIP, SPENCER. THE LAST THING I NEED ARE ANY OF MY PEOPLE LOOKING LIKE FOOLS.
NEXT TIME YOU CALL IN A REPORT ON YOUR MAGICAL, MYSTICAL STREET GANG THAT STEALS USELESS ARTIFACTS, MAKE SURE YOU HAVE THE POWER TO CATCH ONE OF THEM.
YES, SIR.

NOW SORT THIS MESS AND GET OUT OF THAT DRESS. I DON'T KNOW WHETHER TO PRAY WITH YOU OR PRAY FOR YOU.

THE STOCKS WENT UP IN ANTICIPATION OF THE MERGER, WHICH WILL BE OFFICIALLY ANNOUNCED AT A SPEECH TOMORROW IN CENTRAL PARK.
HARLEM, NEW YORK.

BROTHER HOPE HAS HAD GLOBAL ASPIRATIONS FOR SOME TIME AND FOR L.B.C. THE COLLABORATION WITH THE INFLUENTIAL LEADER IS CONSIDERED A VERY PROGRESSIVE MOVE.
ZZZZ

FLAP

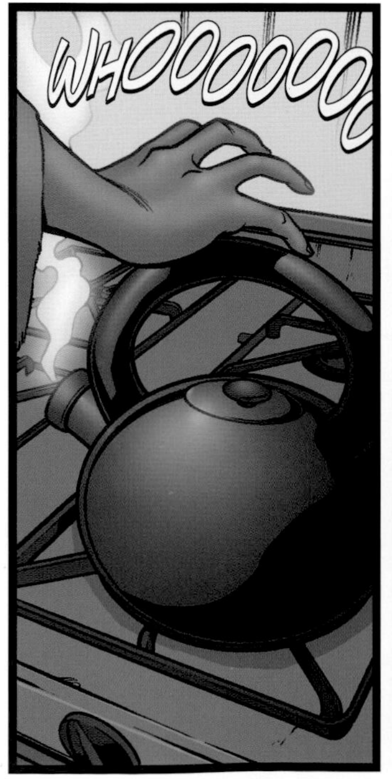
WHOOOOOOO

HELLO, MARIAH.

CLATTER

OH, MY GOODNESS.

MOM, YOU OKAY? *MOM?*

I'M... FINE.
JUST BROKE A CUP.

OH, OKAY. BROOM AND DUST PAN ARE IN THE CLOSET ON THE RIGHT.

NOAH, I CAN'T BELIEVE IT'S YOU.

FOR TWENTY-EIGHT YEARS I WONDERED IF YOU WERE ALIVE.
I WOKE UP AND EVERYTHING HAD CHANGED.
THERE WAS NO MESSAGE, NO NOTHING.
SO YOU FLED AND HOPED NEVER TO BE FOUND.

I CAME TO AMERICA AND AFTER ELIJAH WAS BORN. I JUST KEPT MOVING FROM STATE-TO-STATE AND CITY-TO-CITY TO HIDE OUR TRAIL.
AS THE YEARS PASSED, EVERYTHING SEEMED OKAY. I ASSUMED WE MUST HAVE BEEN FREED BY A BREACH IN THE MAGIC. YOU KNOW–BY ACCIDENT.
I PIECED TOGETHER BITS OF INFORMATION BUT NEVER HAD A *TRUE* UNDERSTANDING OF EXACTLY WHAT HAPPENED.

WHAT'S MOST IRONIC IS WITH ALL YOUR RUNNING, HERE IS YOUR SON, RIGHT UNDER SIRACH'S NOSE.

NO. YOU DON'T--*WAIT.* SIRACH IS HERE?

THERE.
WE'RE COMING TO YOU FROM ONE OF THE BIGGEST PARTIES OF THE YEAR. CELEBRITIES FROM ALL OVER THE CITY HAVE GATHERED IN HONOR OF BROTHER HOPE.

IT IS EXPECTED THAT TOMORROW IN CENTRAL PARK, HOPE WILL MAKE AN EXCITING ANNOUNCEMENT INVOLVING THE L.B.C. SATELLITES.

HE IS BROTHER HOPE?

BROTHER HOPE IS THE PERFECT COVER FOR SOMEONE HIDING A DOCTRINE OF DESTRUCTION.
ALL HE HAS TO DO IS KEEP APPEALING TO THE BASIC NEEDS OF THE MASSES.
WHAT ARE WE GOING TO DO?

ABOUT THAT CUP? C'MON MOM, I'VE BROKEN PLENTY OF YOUR CUPS.

DID YOU FIND THE BROOM?

THAT'S THE BROTHER HOPE YOU WERE ASKING ME ABOUT.
I HOPE TO HAVE HIS INFLUENCE AND POPULARITY ONE DAY.
I'M SO SORRY, ELIJAH.
NO, MOM, IT'S A GOOD THING.
UGH. MOM! YOU DIDN'T-
MOM?

MANHATTAN

IN TODAY'S WORLD PEOPLE ARE MORE FOCUSED ON LOOKING LIKE THEY HAVE MONEY THAN ACTUALLY HAVING MONEY.

THAT'S WHY I PLAN ON SEIZING THIS MOMENT BEFORE THE DISTRICT ATTORNEY IS BACK ON HIS FEET AND I'M YESTERDAY'S NEWS.

ADL-4691

TODAY IS A GOOD DAY TO BE EXTRAORDINARY.

WISH ME LUCK?

MOM?

YES?

OH.

UNITY BANK BUILDING
UNITY
ELIJAH ALEXANDER TO SEE SOPHIA BRONOZ AND THE UNITY GROUP.
BRONOZ, CHAMPION AND KLEIN
ATTORNEYS AT LAW
THEY WILL BE RIGHT WITH YOU.
RINGGG♫
♫RIIINNGGG
Incoming Call
Sydney
YOU CALLING TO WISH ME LUCK?

YOU DON'T NEED IT.
TRUE. BUT IT NEVER HURTS.
THEN I WISH YOU ALL THE SUCCESS IN THE WORLD.
THANKS. SAW THE NEWS THIS MORNING. LAST NIGHT'S MUSEUM HEIST WAS YOU?
IN ALL MY *FAILED* GLORY.
WHAT WAS STOLEN?
ANCIENT NUBIAN CRYSTAL. OLDEST EVER FOUND.
PROBABLY WORTH QUITE A LOT ON THE BLACK MARKET.
THEY WON'T SELL IT.
JUSTICE CENTER

WHY NOT?
ACCORDING TO LEGEND, IT BELONGED TO AN ANCIENT MYSTICAL WARRIOR. IT WAS BELIEVED HE USED THE CRYSTAL TO OPEN DOORS.
TO WHAT?
ALTERNATE DIMENSIONS.

I'M WORRIED ABOUT YOU.
WHY? BECAUSE I BELIEVE A SUPERNATURAL UNDERGROUND CRIME SYNDICATE IS STEALING ANCIENT ARTIFACTS THAT OPEN ALTERNATE DIMENSIONS?
I'M WORRIED ABOUT ME TOO.
UEZ

YOU'RE CUTE WHEN YOU BABBLE ABOUT YOUR MAGICAL STREET GANG.
MR. ALEXANDER, THEY ARE READY FOR YOU NOW.
GOTTA RUN. TALK LATER?
YOU GOT IT.

MS. BRONOZ, AS A PRIVATE CONGLOMERATE OF INFLUENTIAL BUSINESS OWNERS AND COMMUNITY LEADERS, YOUR INTERESTS ARE VARIED AND COMPLEX. HOW CAN YOU BEST CONNECT THE LOWER, MIDDLE *AND* UPPER CLASSES? I OFFER A HIP, FRESH FLAVOR TO SELL YOUR MESSAGE TO WALL STREET.

YOU NEED SOMEONE WHO IS AS EQUALLY COMFORTABLE ON 125TH STREET AS HE IS ON PARK AVENUE IF YOU WANT TO CAPITALIZE ON WHAT IS HAPPENING NOT ONLY IN THIS COUNTRY BUT AROUND THE WORLD.

TAKE A GOOD LOOK LADIES AND GENTLEMEN.

THIS IS THE *FACE OF THE FUTURE.*

PLEASE WELCOME THE MAYOR OF NEW YORK, *MICHELLE TIBBS!*

CENTRAL PARK

TEN YEARS AGO, SOME OF YOU HERE IN THIS PARK WERE HOMELESS. WHAT GAVE YOU SHELTER? HOPE. SEVEN YEARS AGO, MOST OF YOU WERE HUNGRY. WHAT FED YOU? HOPE! FIVE YEARS AGO, SOME OF YOU BROTHERS WERE USING. SOME OF YOU SISTERS WERE BROKEN. WHAT CHANGED YOU? HOPE!

THREE YEARS AGO, SOCIETY HAD YOU AFRAID TO FOLLOW YOUR DREAMS. WHAT INSTILLED CONFIDENCE?

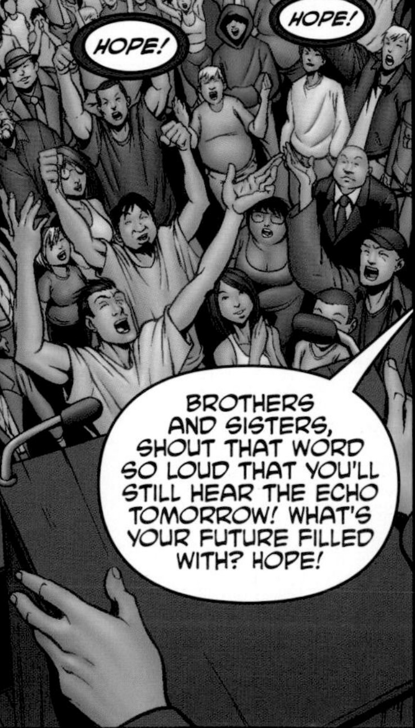
HOPE!
HOPE!
BROTHERS AND SISTERS, SHOUT THAT WORD SO LOUD THAT YOU'LL STILL HEAR THE ECHO TOMORROW! WHAT'S YOUR FUTURE FILLED WITH? HOPE!

HOPE!
HOPE!
HOPE!

MY FRIENDS. I COME BEFORE YOU TODAY ASKING FOR NOTHING AT ALL... EXCEPT YOUR OWN WILLINGNESS TO WITNESS THE POWER TO PRODUCE REAL TRANSFORMATION.
USING THE L.B.C. SATELLITES, ALREADY A MAINSTAY IN NEWS AND MEDIA THROUGHOUT THE U.S. AND EUROPE...

The Hope Network
Building a Better Tomorrow
...THE NEW HOPE NETWORK WILL BE THE *FIRST* LIVE LIFE-AFFIRMING CHANNEL...

...TO REACH HOMES IN PLACES AS FAR AS AFRICA, AUSTRALIA, SOUTH AMERICA, JAPAN...

...AT THE SAME TIME.

TOGETHER, THE HOPE NETWORK IS BUILDING A BETTER TOMORROW.
The Hope Network
Building a Better Tomorrow

HOPE!
HOPE!
HOPE

YOU SHOULD NOT BE HERE.

...
...I HAD TO SEE HIM FOR MYSELF.

HOW MUCH DOES ELIJAH KNOW?
I'VE ONLY TOLD HIM THE TRUTH THROUGH A BOOK OF FOLK TALES.

YOU TURNED THREE THOUSAND YEARS OF HISTORY INTO CHILDHOOD FANTASIES?
WHAT ABOUT HIS POWERS?
I COULD NOT TRAIN HIM SO I SUPPRESSED THEM.

YOU LOST FAITH. YOU DIDN'T BELIEVE.

CAN YOU TELL ME YOU NEVER LOST YOUR WAY?
I DIDN'T AWAKE IN CANDOR'S ARMS.
I RETURNED TO A WORLD I DIDN'T RECOGNIZE. WHAT WAS I SUPPOSED TO DO?

FACE THE CHOICE YOU MADE YEARS AGO.

IT WAS NOT MY--
!

WE MUST GO NOW.

TELL YOUR SON THE TRUTH *TONIGHT* OR *I* WILL.

WE HAVE HIM SURROUNDED.

PROCEED WITH CAUTION.

SPANISH HARLEM

SO I WAS OFFERED A POSITION AT FREAKIN' BRONOZ, CHAMPION AND KLEIN FOR TEN TIMES MY SALARY...BUT ALL I REALLY HAVE TO DO IS SHOW UP.

MOM, THEY'RE GROOMING ME TO BE MAYOR! I SOLD IT! I'VE FINALLY FOUND MY PLACE.

ELIJAH, CAN YOU PULL OVER?

ELIJAH? *MUST* BE SERIOUS.

LOOK MOM, IF THIS IS ABOUT HOW YOU THINK I'VE BECOME TOO SHALLOW, I'M SORRY. BUT NO ONE GAVE US *A THING* WHEN I WAS GROWING UP.

IT WAS ALL ABOUT *THEM.* WELL, NOW IT'S ALL ABOUT *ME.* THIS IS WHO I AM.

FROM WHAT?

I CAN WAIT HERE ALL NIGHT, MOM. RUNNING FROM WHAT?
OUR PAST, YOUR FUTURE.
I DON'T UNDERSTAND.

AS PARENTS WE MAKE CHOICES.

SOMETIMES THEY ARE GOOD AND OTHER TIMES--

I CAN'T DO THIS.

DO WHAT, MOM?

CHUDUDUDUDUDUDUD

MOM, WHERE ARE YOU GOING?
I SAID I WOULD TELL HIM!

ARLITO'S
IAN FOOD
I UNDERSTAND YOUR MISPLACED ANGER, BUT I AM NOT THE ENEMY.

WHO ARE YOU? WERE YOU FOLLOWING US?
I ASKED YOU A QUESTION.

MARIAH.

ELIJAH, EVERY STORY IN YOUR BOOK OF LEGENDS IS REAL.

WHAT ARE YOU TALKING ABOUT?

WHAT YOUR MOTHER SAYS IS TRUE.
MOM, WHO IS THIS GUY?

PERHAPS IT WOULD BE BETTER IF WE TALKED SOMEWHERE ELSE.

NO, SHOW HIM.

MY NAME IS NOAH, YOUR FATHER'S BEST FRIEND AND ENEMY OF SIRACH, THE MAN YOU KNOW AS BROTHER HOPE.

NOAH? SIRACH? YOU'RE JOKING, RIGHT?

THREE THOUSAND YEARS AGO, IN NUBIA, AFRICA, THERE WAS A SPECIAL CITY CALLED *UTOPIA.*
ZAAAAA

SCREEE

I'D HOLD OFF ON THE MAGICAL TRIP DOWN MEMORY LANE, OLD MAN.
GET BEHIND ME.
WHO IS IT?
NEW WORLD KNIGHTS.
WAIT, THEY'RE *REAL?*

TOOK US A WHILE, BUT WE CAUGHT UP. YOU SHOULD REALLY STOP WEARING LONG CLOAKS, NOAH. THE NEIGHBORS TWEET.

GO NOW OR **DIE.**

HEY, *NO!*
WHAT ARE YOU *DOING?*

SURPRISED TO SEE YOU UP AND ABOUT, NOAH.

IF THIS IS BETWEEN YOU GUYS LET ME--

I WILL RIP THE SPINE FROM YOUR BACK BEFORE I TELL YOU AGAIN.
WHAT IS *WRONG* WITH YOU?

LOOK, I DON'T KNOW WHAT'S GOING ON HERE OR WHO YOU GUYS ARE BUT MY MOTHER AND I DON'T WANT ANY TROUBLE.

ELIJAH. TAKE YOUR MOTHER AND LEAVE.
THANK YOU. LET'S GO MOM.

SORRY, BUT YOU'RE *ALL* COMING WITH US.

LISTEN, MY NAME IS ELIJAH ALEXANDER AND I'M AN ASSISTANT DISTRICT ATTORNEY.
YOU DON'T WANT TO DO ANYTHING YOU'LL REGRET!

REGRET? THIS IS WHAT WE LIVE FOR!

GUYS WAIT!
MARIAH...
MOM.
MOM?
FWISH
CHOOOM
NOW!
GUH!
BLAM
CHOOM
OOF!
GACK!
CHOOM
GO!
GO!
ZRSHH

TNK
TNK
TNK

tnk
tnk
tnk
tnk
ZAKOOM

SWAASHH
GAH!
AHH!

NYAA!
UNH!
YAAH!
SWAASHH
GET THE OTHER TWO!

DOWN THIS ALLY!
BLAM
BLAM
BLAM

FWOOSH
DEAD END! WE'RE TRAPPED.
STEP BACK.

HOW ARE YOU--?
THIS WAY, HURRY.

COME OUT! COME OUT!

CLANG
CLANG

THEY'RE OVER BY THOSE CARS!

THOOM
UNH.

HOW ARE YOU DOING THAT?
I AM SOMETHING WHICH YOU DON'T THINK EXISTS.
YOU'RE A-

SANCTUANT.
AND THAT MAKES ME-

THE LAST MANTAMAJI.

BWOOSH
HUNH!

BLAM
BLAM
CHOOM
CHOOM
AGH!
NYA!

STAY BEHIND ME.
YAAAHH!
CHOOM
MOM, WAIT.

RAARGH!

HEY! HEY! HEY!
ZAASSH
GKK!

CHOOOM
UNH!
CHOOM

BLAM
RAAH!
HYA!

THOOM

YOU KILLED THEM!
BROKE TWELVE RIBS, THREE ARMS AND TWO LEGS, BUT THEY'LL LIVE.
IF YOU COULD DO ALL THAT, WHY DID WE RUN?
BECAUSE *YOU* CAN'T. LET'S GO.
YES MA'AM.
TO BE CONTINUED

CHAPTER 3

With a flash of light the knights would swarm out of the night air, with the fury of a thousand simooms. Like those sandstorms, they were everywhere: unstoppable, inescapable, devastating their foes in moments before vanishing again...

YOU REMEMBER THE STORY...

3000 YEARS AGO

THREE THOUSAND YEARS AGO A SELECT GROUP OF HUMANS WERE BORN WITH MAGIC POWERS TO HELP PROTECT THIS WORLD...

...FROM THE FORCES OF EVIL.

CANDOR...
...NOAH...
...AND SIRACH...
...WERE THE FIERCEST OF ALL THESE WARRIORS....

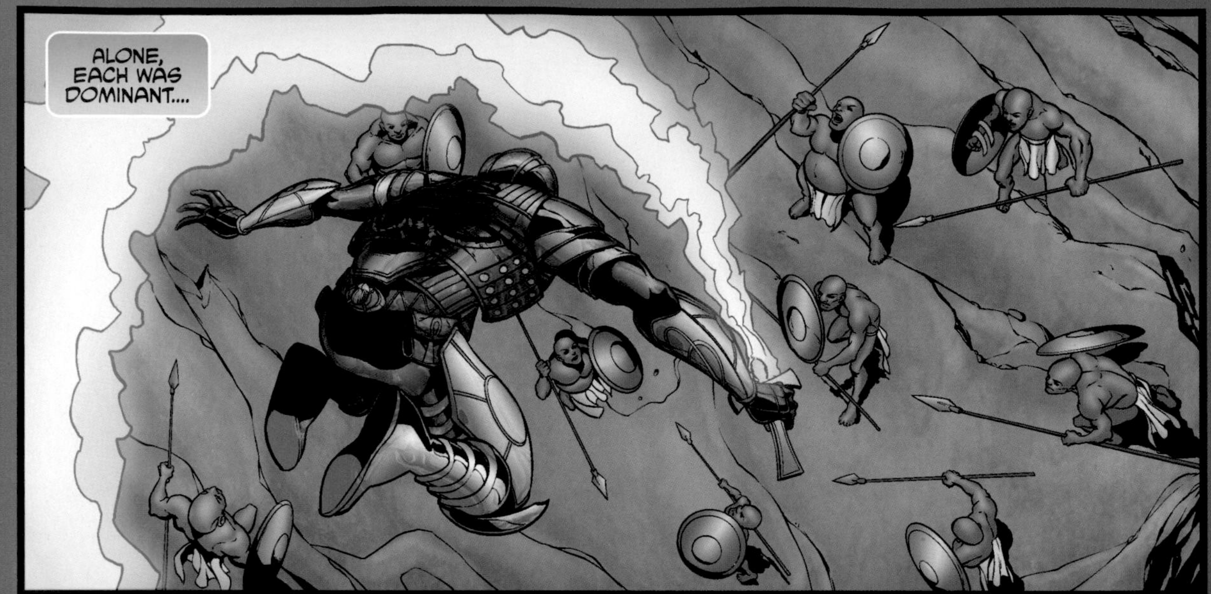
ALONE, EACH WAS DOMINANT....

TOGETHER, THEY WERE UNSTOPPABLE.

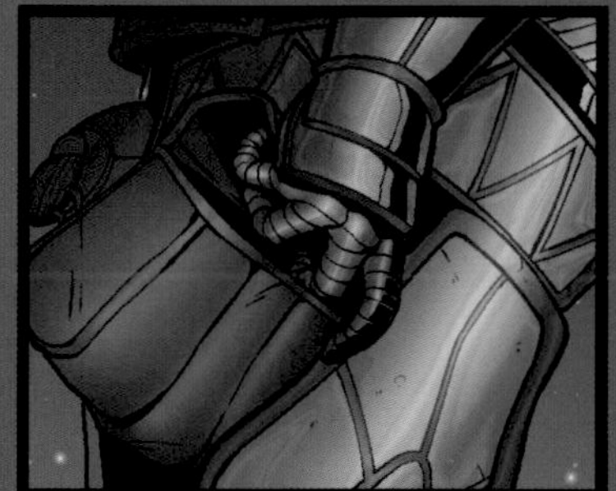

ENDOWED WITH A MAGICAL CRYSTAL, THEY COVERED THE GLOBE AS EARTH'S GREATEST PROTECTORS.

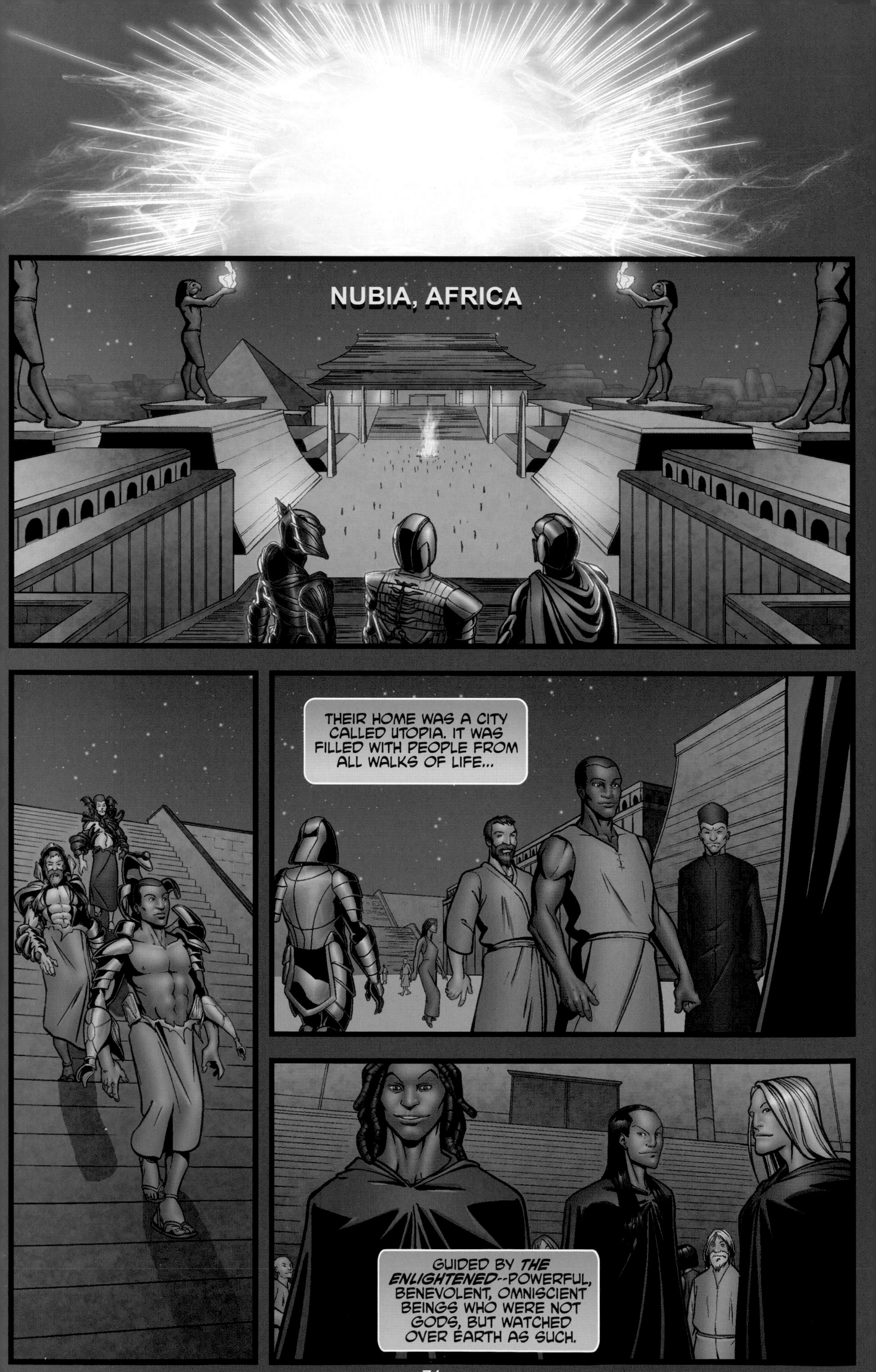

NUBIA, AFRICA

THE ENLIGHTENED BELIEVED SO DEEPLY AND STRONGLY IN HUMANS THAT THEY UNITED WITH MANKIND TO FORM SPECIAL BEINGS.

THE FIRST-BORN MALE CHILD OF THESE CHOSEN ONES WAS CALLED A MANTAMAJI.

THE FIRST-BORN FEMALE CHILD WAS CALLED A SANCTUANT.
DAD!

AND AS THE MANTAMAJI AND SANCTUANTS UNITED, THEIR FIRST-BORN WOULD FOLLOW SUIT, GIVING BIRTH TO ONE OF EACH LIKE THEM.

FWOOOSH
WHERE THE MANTAMAJI WERE SOLDIERS, THE SANCTUANTS WERE MYSTICAL BEINGS GIFTED WITH THE ABILITY TO CONJURE BIOGENIC ENERGY WITH THEIR HANDS.

ROOAHHR

TOGETHER THEY FORMED THE PERFECT UNION. *HEROES,* NOBLE, STRONG, FULL OF LOVE, STRENGTH AND THE *POWER OF THE SOUL...*

...BUT STILL HALF HUMAN.

MEANING THEY WERE PRONE TO MAKING MISTAKES.

AT THE COUNCIL OF ENLIGHTENMENT

WE HAVE GROWN TIRED OF THE SACRIFICE MADE TO PROTECT HUMANITY.

WHOM DO YOU SPEAK FOR, SIRACH?

WHAT IF I COULD *MAKE IT PERFECT,* CANDOR?

PERFECT FOR WHO? *YOU?* OURS IS NOT TO QUESTION DIVINE RIGHT.

WE WERE BESTOWED WITH GIFTS THAT MUST BE USED FOR GOOD.

SIRACH LEFT US BECAUSE HE REFUSED TO EMBRACE THE SIMPLE TRUTH THAT A HERO'S LIFE IS ONE OF SACRIFICE.

I WILL USE MY POWERS AS I SEE FIT.

THIS IS WHAT I'VE NEVER TOLD YOU...
ONE YEAR LATER

FWAP

SHOOOM
SHOOOM
SHOOOM
FWAP
AIIEEEE!
FWAP
BWOOSH
NNGK!
BWOOSH

SHOOOM

MARIAH.

CANDOR! OH THANK THE HEAVENS IT'S YOU. WHAT IS HAPPENING?

BWOOOSH

SIRACH HAS RETURNED.
HOW DID HE GET SO POWERFUL?
WE DON'T KNOW, BUT I MUST GET YOU TO SAFETY.

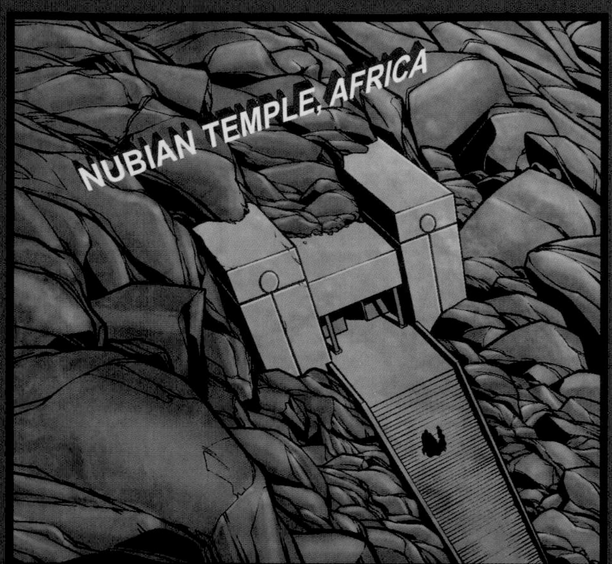
NUBIAN TEMPLE, AFRICA

WHAT IS THIS PLACE?
YOUR NEW HOME.

NOAH, WHAT DO YOU MEAN?
WHAT IS HE TALKING ABOUT, CANDOR?

ALL THE MANTAMAJI HAVE RETURNED. YOUNG AND OLD. WE ARE GATHERING TO FIGHT SIRACH AND HIS ARMY AT THE GATES OF THE CITY BUT WE MUST HAVE SOME ASSURANCE THE MANTAMAJI WILL LIVE ON.

NO. I WANT TO STAY WITH BOTH OF YOU AND FIGHT.
YOU ARE IN NO CONDITION TO DO THAT.
YOUR UNBORN BABY HAS BEEN CHOSEN.

NOAH, WHY CAN'T YOUR SON BE THE ONE? HE IS ALREADY SO GIFTED.
JOSHUA AWAITS ON THE FRONT LINE.
THE CHOSEN ONE MUST BE SOMEONE WHO HAS NOT SET FOOT IN THIS WORLD.
SIRACH HAS KILLED THE ENLIGHTENED.
NO! BUT IF SIRACH IS THIS POWERFUL, WHAT POSSIBLE LOGIC IS THERE FOR A MANTAMAJI NOT EVEN YET BORN TO BE LOCKED AWAY?
HOW CAN HE MAKE A DIFFERENCE?

IF SIRACH DOES DEFEAT US, AN UNBORN CHILD IS THE ONLY MANTAMAJI HIS MAGIC CANNOT DETECT. AS MUCH AS I WANT YOU BY MY SIDE, WE HAVE TO LEAVE THE WORLD A GLIMMER OF HOPE.

GOODBYE MARIAH. CANDOR, WHEN WE MEET AGAIN...
LET IT BE IN VICTORY.
LET IT BE IN VICTORY.

COME SISTERS, WE MUST MOVE QUICKLY.

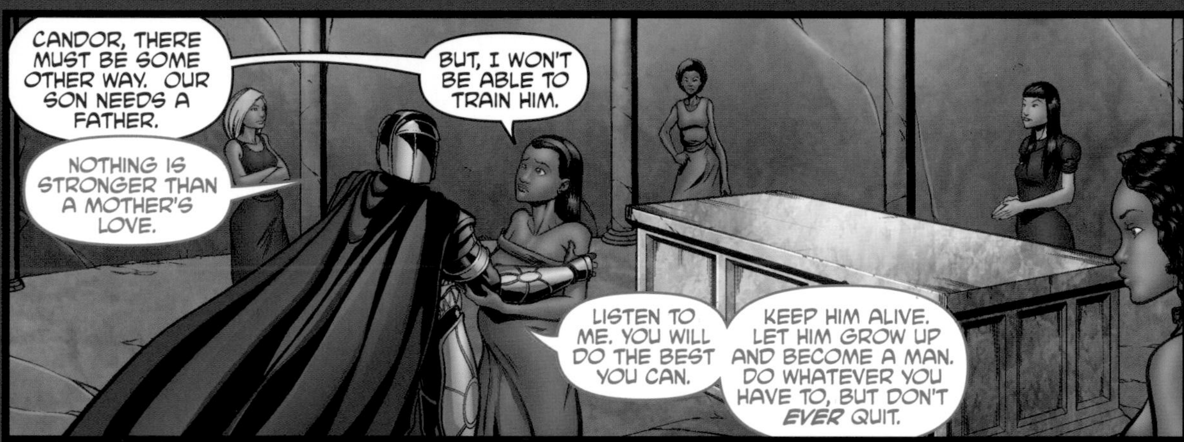
CANDOR, THERE MUST BE SOME OTHER WAY. OUR SON NEEDS A FATHER.
BUT, I WON'T BE ABLE TO TRAIN HIM.
NOTHING IS STRONGER THAN A MOTHER'S LOVE.
LISTEN TO ME. YOU WILL DO THE BEST YOU CAN.
KEEP HIM ALIVE. LET HIM GROW UP AND BECOME A MAN. DO WHATEVER YOU HAVE TO, BUT DON'T EVER QUIT.

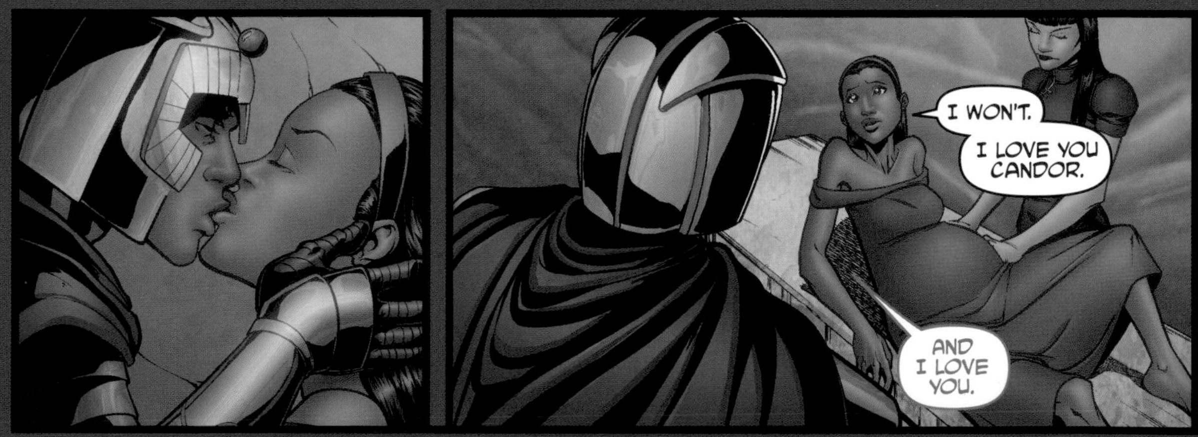
I WON'T.
I LOVE YOU CANDOR.
AND I LOVE YOU.

WE COMMIT OUR SOULS TO THIS MOTHER AND UNBORN CHILD.

LET THEM REST PEACEFULLY UNTIL THAT DAY WHEN OUR DESCENDANTS CALL UPON THEM AGAIN.
ONCE WE WERE PUT TO REST I NEVER KNEW WHAT HAPPENED, BUT I HAD TO BELIEVE YOUR FATHER SOMEHOW SAVED HUMANITY, BECAUSE WHEN I AWOKE, THE WORLD WAS NOT UNDER SIRACH'S RULE.

ELIJAH'S BROWNSTONE TWO NIGHTS AGO.
FOR YOU, I MADE THESE STORIES AND IMAGES CHILDHOOD FAIRY TALES. BUT THEY ARE REALLY OUR FAMILY PHOTO ALBUM.

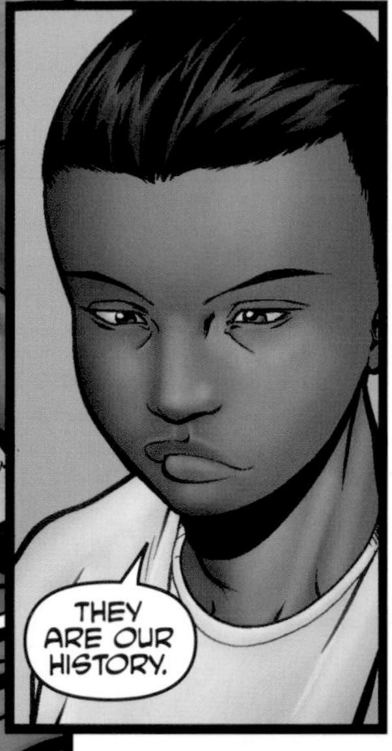

THEY ARE OUR HISTORY.

DING DONG

NOAH.

ARE YOU OKAY?

I HAD TO CLEAN UP THE MESS.

I'M SORRY. I JUST WANTED TO GET ELIJAH OUT OF THERE.

SO...

...YOU'RE BOTH OVER THREE THOUSAND YEARS OLD?

MORE OR LESS.
LESS.

BUT WHAT DO THESE STORIES HAVE TO DO WITH WHAT HAPPENED TONIGHT?

UTOPIA, AFRICA
3000 YEARS AGO

AFTER YOU AND MARIAH WERE PUT IN AN ETERNAL SLEEP, THE MANTAMAJI GATHERED AT THE GATES OF UTOPIA TO FIGHT AGAINST SIRACH FOR THE SURVIVAL OF ALL MANKIND.

SWAASSH

HYA!

WHOOSH

YAA!

NOOOOOOOO!!
WE LOST EVERYONE WE EVER CARED ABOUT.

AND IN THE END, ONLY A FEW OF US SURVIVED.

UNABLE TO WATCH THE CARNAGE ANY LONGER.

FORGIVE ME, MY LOVE.

CANDOR MADE A BRAVE BUT TRAGIC CHOICE.

SIRACH, YOU MUST STOP THIS WAR.

IT COMES DOWN TO YOU AND ME, CANDOR. JUST AS IT SHOULD BE. JOIN ME AND TOGETHER WE CAN FIX THIS WORLD.

YOU DON'T WANT TO REPAIR, SIRACH. YOU WANT TO *RULE*.

I'M GOING TO CREATE A *NEW UTOPIA*. I JUST NEED YOUR TRANSPORTATION CRYSTAL TO BE THE BRIDGE.

THIS WAS BESTOWED UPON ME TO ALLOW US TO PROTECT MANKIND, NOT DESTROY US ALL.

I WILL USE IT TO *SAVE* US ALL.

WHAT YOU ARE TRYING TO DO IS GENOCIDE.

NO MY FRIEND.
IT IS *THE FUTURE.*

SHKNNNNN

UGH!

I'M TOO STRONG.

YOU'VE LOST, CANDOR.

SO HAVE *YOU.*

HUNH!

!

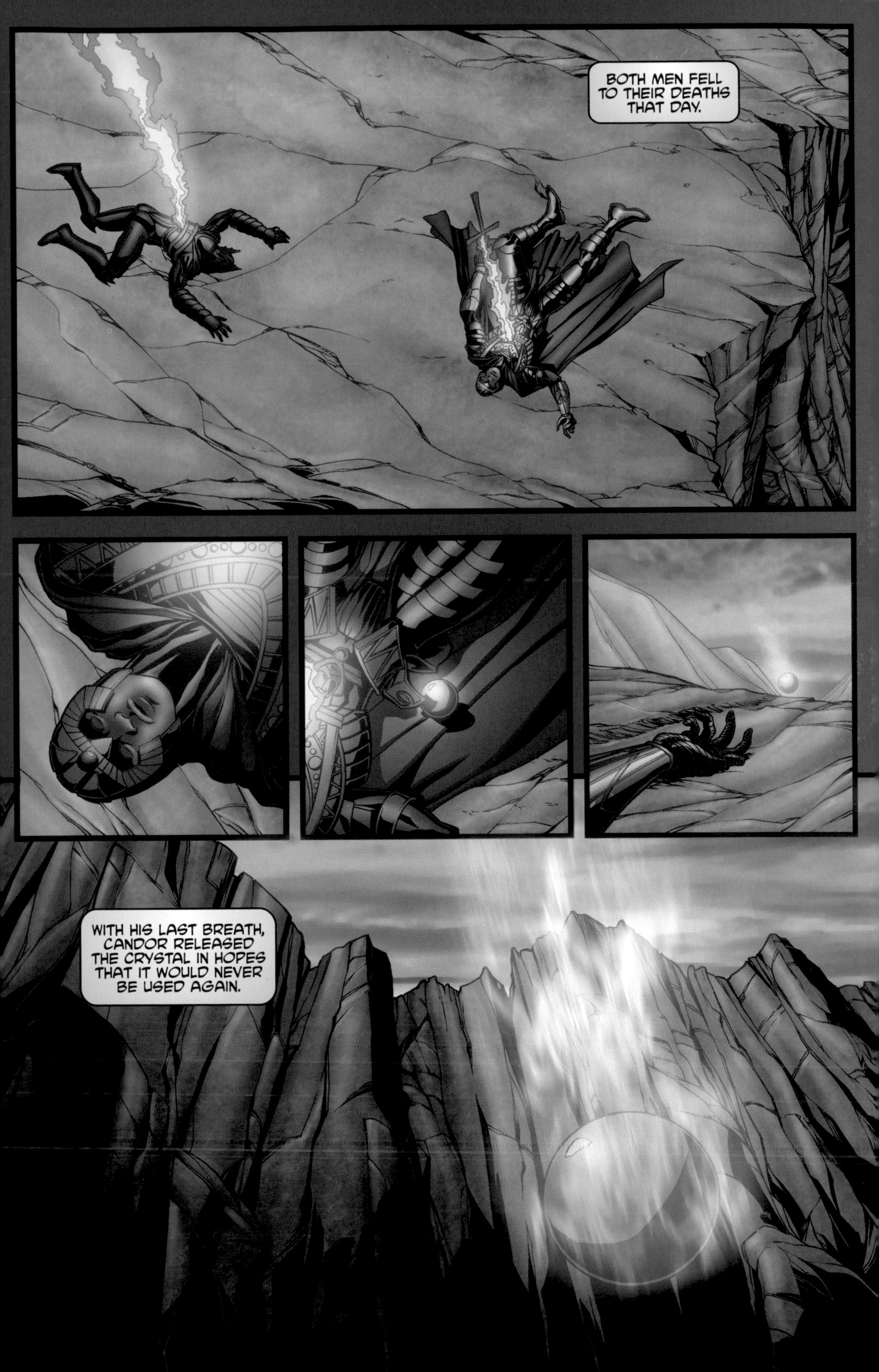
BOTH MEN FELL TO THEIR DEATHS THAT DAY.
WITH HIS LAST BREATH, CANDOR RELEASED THE CRYSTAL IN HOPES THAT IT WOULD NEVER BE USED AGAIN.

GREECE 580 A.D.
ALTHOUGH WE WON THE BATTLE WITH SIRACH, THE WAR HAD JUST BEGUN.
SIRACH'S FOLLOWERS FORMED SECRET SOCIETIES.
FOR EVERY HUNDRED YEARS, ON THE ANNIVERSARY OF HIS DEATH, A CELESTIAL ALIGNMENT WOULD ALLOW THEIR BLOOD TO BRING SIRACH BACK TO LIFE.

JOINED BY THE REMAINING SANCTUANTS, WE TRAVELED THE GLOBE, CONTINUING THE FIGHT.

CHUD
CHUD
CHUD

ZWAAAASSH

WE MOVED QUIETLY THROUGH THE CENTURIES.
FLORENCE, ITALY 1280 A.D.
LIVING IN SECRET.
WITH ONE GOAL IN MIND.
WHENEVER THEY WOULD RISE, WHEREVER THEY WOULD BE, WE WOULD *FIND* THEM.
AND RAIN DOWN *VENGEANCE FOR ALL MANKIND.*
KRAAASSH

HARLEM, NEW YORK. 28 YEARS AGO.
WE HAD REDUCED THEIR NUMBERS TO THE POINT WHERE WE WERE POISED TO WIPE THEM FROM THE EARTH, ONCE AND FOR ALL, BUT THEY STILL HAD ONE ADVANTAGE.
TO BE A SUCCESS FIGHTING TERRORISM, YOU HAVE TO GET IT RIGHT EVERY SINGLE TIME. UNFORTUNATELY, THE TERRORIST ONLY NEEDS TO GET IT RIGHT ONCE.
THROUGH THE CENTURIES WE HAD FOUND THEIR MESSAGE DROPS, CRACKED THEIR CODES, TAPPED THEIR LANDLINES, BUT OUR POWERS WERE BASED IN MAGIC, NOT TECHNOLOGY. HACKING INTO THEIR COMPUTER NETWORK REVEALED THAT THEY HAD SET UP A RESURRECTION POINT IN AN ABANDONED BUILDING IN NEW YORK.
WE ATTACKED FROM ALL ANGLES WITH PRECISION AND PURPOSE.
BLAM
BLAM
BLAM
OOF!
ZZZZZ

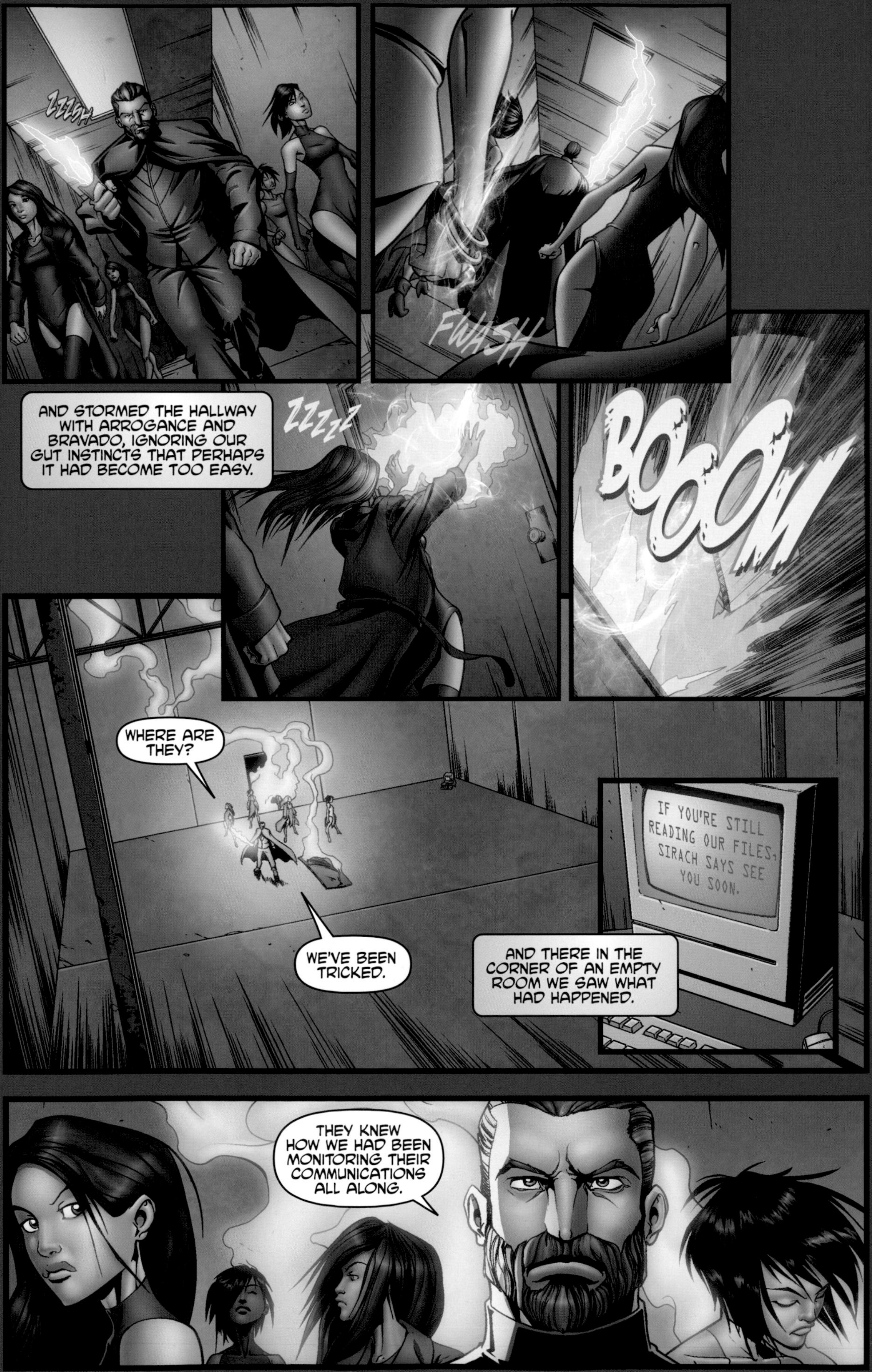

ZZZSH

FWASH

AND STORMED THE HALLWAY WITH ARROGANCE AND BRAVADO, IGNORING OUR GUT INSTINCTS THAT PERHAPS IT HAD BECOME TOO EASY.

ZZZZZ

BOOOOM

WHERE ARE THEY?

WE'VE BEEN TRICKED.

IF YOU'RE STILL READING OUR FILES, SIRACH SAYS SEE YOU SOON.

AND THERE IN THE CORNER OF AN EMPTY ROOM WE SAW WHAT HAD HAPPENED.

ZSSSH
THOUSANDS OF LIVES LOST CHASING HIS DISCIPLES ACROSS THE GLOBE HAD ALL BEEN UNDONE IN A SINGLE MOMENT.

THREE MILLENNIA AFTER CANDOR LAID HIM DOWN, SIRACH WALKED THE EARTH ONCE MORE.

I HAVE SPENT **EVERY HOUR** SINCE THAT NIGHT LOOKING FOR BOTH OF YOU.

I'M SO, **SO SORRY.**

IT'S NOT YOUR FAULT MOM.
AGREED. NOW IS NOT THE TIME TO PLACE BLAME. WE MUST STOP SIRACH.

GOOD LUCK WITH THAT.

WHAT DO YOU MEAN?
EXACTLY WHAT IT SOUNDED LIKE. WE CAN'T GET INVOLVED IN THIS.

YOU HAVE TO.

NO. I *DON'T.*

I DIDN'T RAISE YOU TO BE LIKE THIS.
YOU *DIDN'T* RAISE ME TO BE WHAT YOU SAY I'M *SUPPOSED* TO BE.

I WAS PROTECTING YOU.

THAT'S RIGHT. AND NOW YOU WANT TO THROW ALL THAT AWAY?

YOU HAVE INCREDIBLE POWER INSIDE YOU.
IT'S TIME YOU DISCOVERED IT.

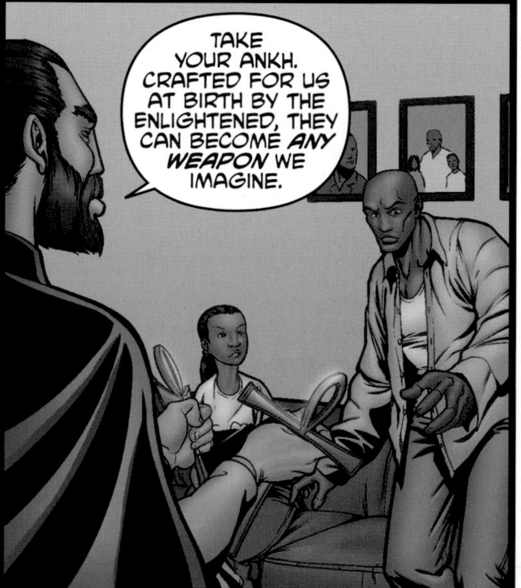
TAKE YOUR ANKH. CRAFTED FOR US AT BIRTH BY THE ENLIGHTENED, THEY CAN BECOME *ANY WEAPON* WE IMAGINE.

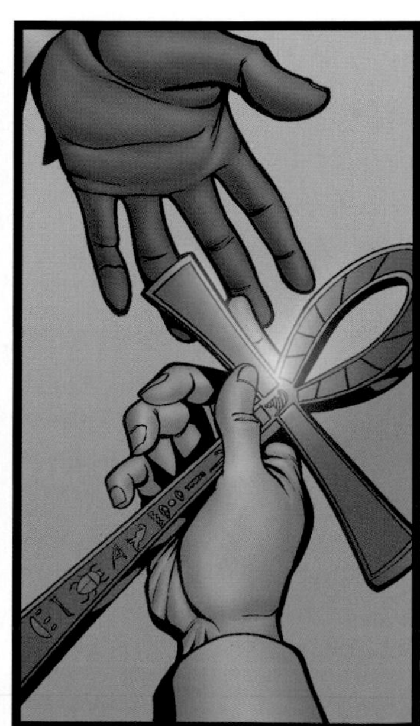

BUT ONLY WHEN WE ARE ONE WITH THE FIRE IN OUR SOUL, WILL IT BECOME A FLAMING SWORD.
VWOOOM

IT'S GOING TO TAKE MORE THAN SOME *CHEAP MAGIC TRICKS* TO CONVINCE *ME* THAT I'M THE *ONLY* GUY STOPPING THE WORLD FROM COMING TO AN END.

OKAY, HOW ABOUT... *THIS!*

HOLY!!
VWOOOSH

WE CAN ALSO CREATE ILLUSIONS, BUT THAT'S FOR A LATER LESSON.

ARE YOU CRAZY?

ELIJAH, NOAH IS HERE TO HELP.
LOOK AT WHAT YOU DID WITH YOUR ANKH.
HE *KNOWS* WHAT HE'S DOING.

WHAT *ARE* YOU DOING?

GIVING HIM PROOF.

FIRST. TURN THAT THING *OFF* BEFORE YOU BURN THIS PLACE DOWN!

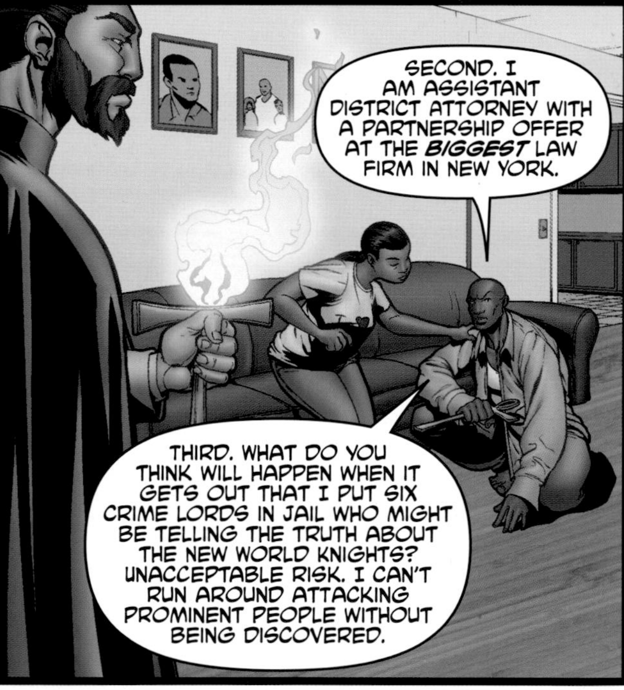
SECOND. I AM ASSISTANT DISTRICT ATTORNEY WITH A PARTNERSHIP OFFER AT THE *BIGGEST* LAW FIRM IN NEW YORK.
THIRD. WHAT DO YOU THINK WILL HAPPEN WHEN IT GETS OUT THAT I PUT SIX CRIME LORDS IN JAIL WHO MIGHT BE TELLING THE TRUTH ABOUT THE NEW WORLD KNIGHTS? UNACCEPTABLE RISK. I CAN'T RUN AROUND ATTACKING PROMINENT PEOPLE WITHOUT BEING DISCOVERED.

YOUR BODY ARMOR WILL PROVIDE THE DISGUISE YOU NEED.
YOU MAKE THIS SOUND EASY. I'M GONNA NEED SOME TIME TO THINK.

WE DON'T *HAVE* TIME.

WHAT'S THE RUSH?

SIRACH RECENTLY GAINED POSSESSION OF YOUR FATHER'S CRYSTAL.
THAT MUCH POWER IN HIS HANDS COULD BE CATASTROPHIC.
COULD BE? THIS IS TOO BIG A DECISION TO BE MADE ON *POSSIBILITIES.* GET BACK TO ME WHEN YOU HAVE *CONCRETE EVIDENCE.*

IT IS YOUR *DESTINY* TO JOIN ME.
MY *DESTINY* IS A SEVEN FIGURE SALARY WITH A CORNER OFFICE OVERLOOKING PARK AVENUE.
THIS IS *MADNESS.*
FOR YEARS MARIAH HID THIS FROM YOU, YET HERE YOU STAND, WORKING IN A CITY WHERE YOUR TRUE ENEMY RESIDES.
DESTINY IS NOT A MATTER OF *CHANCE.* IT IS A MATTER OF *CHOICE.*
IT'S TIME YOU MADE YOURS.
TO BE CONTINUED

CHAPTER 4

If the Mantamaji had doubts about the danger, they kept it to themselves. For all we knew, they had wild, passionate hearts to match their bold clothing. If any among them doubted, all we saw on the outside was the pure brightness of a winter moon.

JUSTICE CENTER
SYDNEY'S OFFICE
TWO DAYS AGO
DETECTIVE SYDNEY SPENCER
SYDNEY, YOU HERE?
OF COURSE NOT.

DID YOU GROW UP AND FIND OUT THE BEDTIME STORIES YOUR MOM TOLD YOU WERE...
CREEEAK

REAL.
WHAT?
THE STATUE. IT'S A REAL AZTEC CARVING. ONE OF A KIND.
...RIGHT.

SO IS THIS A VISIT FROM THE ASSISTANT D.A. OR MY BOYFRIEND?
LITTLE OF BOTH.
INTRIGUING, GO ON?
DO YOU BELIEVE IN FATE?

I BELIEVE WE ARE ALL PUT HERE FOR A REASON. I WAS ABANDONED AT TWO YEARS OLD. WHEN I WAS EIGHT, I SLEPT IN THE BACK OF A CAR IN A JUNK YARD. AT FOURTEEN I DID THINGS I STILL CAN'T TALK ABOUT.

BUT I ALWAYS HOPED THERE WAS SOMETHING MORE FOR ME. WHEN I WAS SIXTEEN, STAYING AT PROBABLY MY TWENTY-THIRD FOSTER HOME, I CALLED THE COPS ON A DRUG DEALER WHO HAD TWO OF THE GIRLS IN THE HOUSE STRUNG OUT. NOT THE RIGHT MOVE.

I BET.

THE DEALER GOT PISSED. I WAS BEATEN UP IN SCHOOL AND THE FAMILY I WAS STAYING WITH WAS THREATENED FOR MEDDLING IN HIS BUSINESS.

AFRAID FOR THEIR LIVES, THE FAMILY THREW ME OUT BECAUSE ME AND MY BIG MOUTH HAD MADE THEM A TARGET.

YOU'RE LUCKY ALL HE DID WAS THREATEN THEM.
THAT'S WHAT I THOUGHT TOO. BUT THEN SOMETHING HAPPENED.

MY PHONE CALL PUT THE DRUG DEALER ON THE D.E.A.'S RADAR.
THEY WERE ABLE TO TRACK HIM BACK TO A MUCH LARGER SUPPLIER AND TOOK DOWN AN ENTIRE OPERATION.
THAT MOMENT DEFINED ME. I BECAME THE PERSON WHO WAS NOT AFRAID TO FIGHT WHEN EVERYONE ELSE WAS. NO MATTER HOW BAD MY LIFE WAS, I COULD NO LONGER NOT GET INVOLVED.

BUT WHAT IF YOUR PHONE CALL DIDN'T TURN OUT THE WAY IT HAD?

IT WASN'T THE CALL THAT CHANGED MY LIFE. IT WAS THE CHOICE TO MAKE THE CALL.
CARING ISN'T FUTILE. TRYING TO HELP PEOPLE GETS RESULTS. DO THE RIGHT THING AND EVERYTHING FALLS INTO PLACE.

I LOST MY CYNICISM... THEN I BECAME A COP AND GOT IT BACK AGAIN, BUT THAT'S ANOTHER STORY.
BEEP
BEEP

COME ON, PICK UP. PICK UP.

BZZZZ BZZZZ

THIS IS MARIAH. I CAN'T TAKE YOUR CALL RIGHT NOW BUT PLEASE LEAVE ME A MESSAGE AND HAVE A BLESSED DAY.

WHERE IS HE NOW?
YOU NEED TO GIVE HIM SOME SPACE.
YOU DON'T KNOW WHAT IT WAS LIKE FOR HIM GROWING UP FEELING DIFFERENT, BUT NOT KNOWING WHY. WE WERE ALWAYS MOVING. IT MADE HIM AN OUTSIDER. THAT NEVER GOES AWAY.
STRIVING TO GET AHEAD IS THE ONLY THING THAT MADE HIM FEEL NORMAL AND NOW HE FINDS OUT IT'S ALL A BIG LIE.

I FEEL FOR HIS PLIGHT IN THESE MODERN TIMES, BUT THERE WERE SACRIFICES MADE FOR HIM.
HE KNOWS WHAT THE MANTAMAJI DID.
BUT NOT WHAT YOUR SISTERS SURRENDERED.

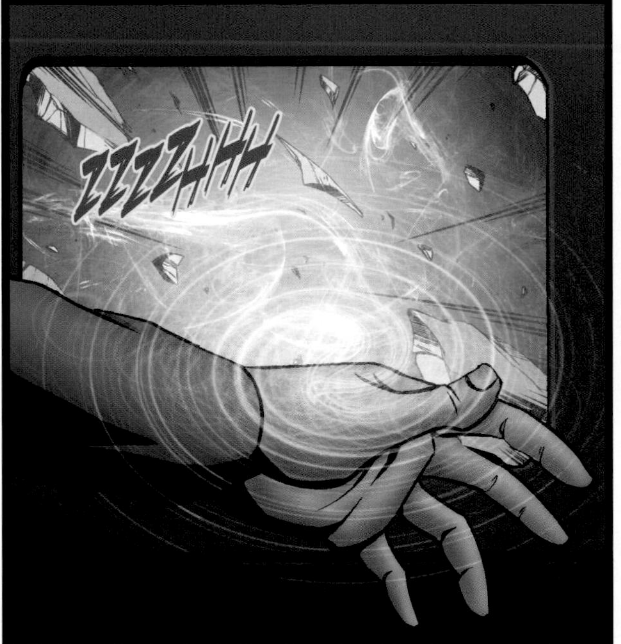
ZZZZHHH

AFTER THE GREAT WAR, BY THE GRACE OF THE ENLIGHTNENED, WE FOUND THAT SANCTUANTS COULD STILL GIVE BIRTH TO SANCTUANTS. THE ELDERS TRAINED THEIR CHILDREN TO USE THEIR SPELLS TO BECOME AN ARMY OF HUNTERS.

ASSASSINS THAT, THROUGHOUT HISTORY, I WOULD LEAD INTO BATTLE.

CHOOOM

BUT AFTER SIRACH WAS RESURRECTED I SET OUT FOR AFRICA TO FIND YOU, FORCING THE SANCTUANTS TO CARRY OUT THEIR OATH.
UPSTATE NEW YORK

WHAT OATH?

WE ARE THE VESSEL. FREE HER FROM THE DIMENSION WHERE SHE RESTS. GUIDE HER BACK TO US HEALTH AND WHOLE.

SSSHHHHHH

SHAWOOOSH

THOOOM
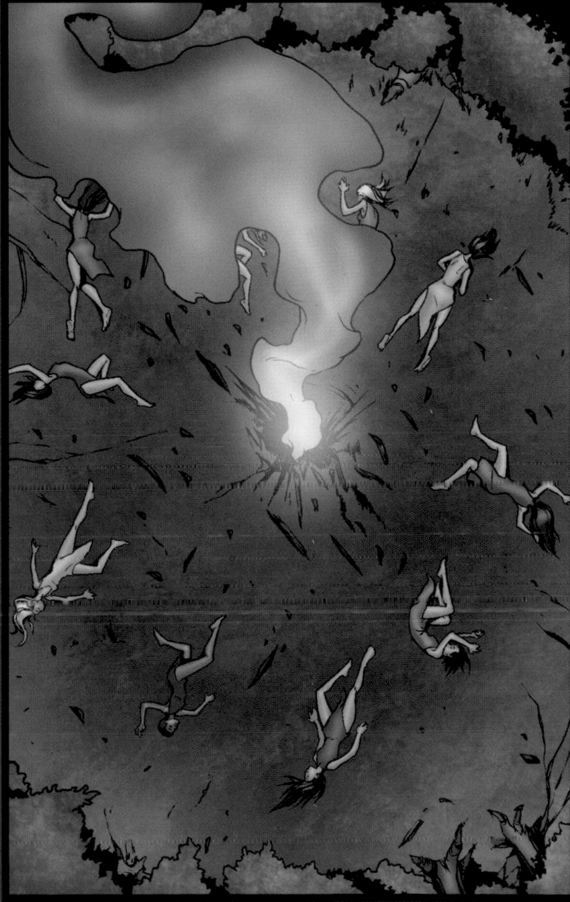

NUBIA, AFRICA.
I WAS SUPPOSED TO BE THERE WHEN YOU AWOKE, BUT UNFORTUNATELY, RECREATING THREE THOUSAND YEAR OLD SPELLS FROM A CONTINENT AWAY IS NOT AN EXACT SCIENCE.
!

ZSHHHH

CHOOOOOM
BY THE TIME I ARRIVED AT YOUR TOMB, YOU WERE GONE.

CORNERSTONE!

CORNERSTONE! COME BACK!

AND THAT IS HOW YOU RETURNED. IT WAS NOT A BREACH IN THE MAGIC. IT WAS ON THE SACRIFICE OF OTHERS TO SAVE MANKIND.

THE SANCTUANTS GAVE THEIR LIVES AND LEFT THEIR CHILDREN TO BRING YOU BACK.
ZAAA

NO, IT CAN'T BE. THOSE CHILDREN. WHAT HAPPENED TO THEM? WHERE ARE THEY?

I PLACED THE YOUNGEST IN ORPHANAGES OR WITH THEIR HUMAN FATHERS IF THEIR POWERS HAD NOT MANIFESTED.

THE TEENAGERS TRIED TO CARRY ON THE FIGHT, BUT WERE NO MATCH FOR SIRACH AND HIS ARMY.

SLISSHH
krik
AHAHAHA
HAHAHA
EVENTUALLY, I LOST CONTACT WITH ALL BUT ONE OF THEM.

ELIJAH CAN'T END UP THE SAME WAY. HE HAS NO TRAINING. THAT IS WHY EVERY MOMENT HE IS NOT HERE IS A WASTE OF TIME.

THIS HAS TO END. I MUST TALK TO HIM NOW!

TAXI!
619

WHERE TO, MA'AM?
BROTHER HOPE'S TEMPLE.
GREENWICH VILLAGE? SURE THING.

BZZZZ
BZZZZ

MOM, I NEED TO TALK TO NOAH. CALL ME AS SOON AS YOU GET THIS MESSAGE.

THERE YOU ARE. YOU HAVE TO GET TO THE WHARF.
MY GIRLFRIEND'S A COP AND SHE KNOWS ABOUT THE NEW WORLD KNIGHTS.

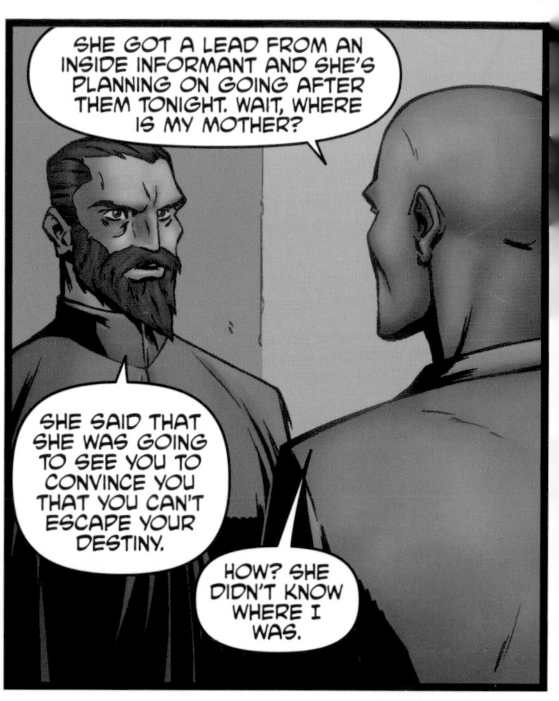
SHE GOT A LEAD FROM AN INSIDE INFORMANT AND SHE'S PLANNING ON GOING AFTER THEM TONIGHT. WAIT, WHERE IS MY MOTHER?
SHE SAID THAT SHE WAS GOING TO SEE YOU TO CONVINCE YOU THAT YOU CAN'T ESCAPE YOUR DESTINY.
HOW? SHE DIDN'T KNOW WHERE I WAS.

OH, NO MARIAH! SHE SAID 'I MUST TALK TO HIM.' I ASSUMED SHE MEANT YOU.
I'M AFRAID NOW SHE MUST HAVE MEANT...THAT SHE'S GONE TO CONFRONT SIRACH.

THAT'S *CRAZY.* WHY WOULD SHE DO THAT?

BECAUSE SHE LOVES YOU AND YOU REFUSED TO ACCEPT YOUR CALLING.

I HAVE TO STOP HER.

SIRACH HAS DEFEATED ME MANY TIMES. YOU'RE NOT EVEN CLOSE TO READY.
I HAVE TO TRY. I CAN'T LET MY MOTHER TAKE ON THAT MADMAN ALONE.

ALLOW ME TO RETRIEVE HER. IT'S THE BEST WAY.
I'LL INTERCEPT YOUR MOTHER AT SIRACH'S TEMPLE. YOU HAD BETTER GET TO THE WHARF. IF SIRACH AND HIS FOLLOWERS ARE HEADED THAT WAY, THEN YOUR POLICE FRIEND IS GOING TO NEED ALL THE HELP SHE CAN GET.
TAKE HER PHONE. I'LL CALL YOU AS SOON AS I GET TO SYDNEY.
AND I'LL CALL YOU WHEN I LOCATE MARIAH.

YOU'VE REACHED DETECTIVE SYDNEY SPENCER'S CELL PHONE, PLEASE LEAVE A MESSAGE. IF THIS IS AN ACTUAL EMERGENCY, HANG UP AND DIAL 911.
SYDNEY, CALL ME! PLEASE!

HOPE'S TEMPLE

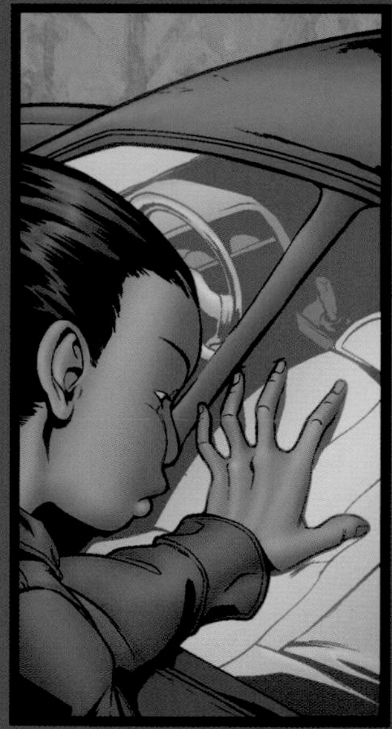

KRSHHH

WEEOOO
WEEOOO
WEEOOO
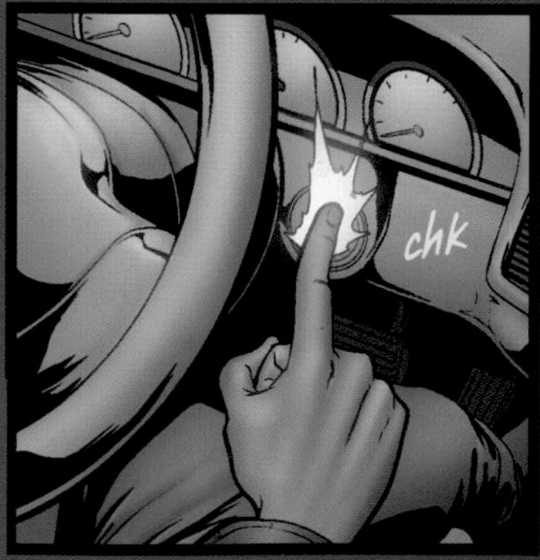
chk

MANHATTAN HARBOR

DISPATCH, THIS IS DETECTIVE SPENCER. I NEED BACKUP AT FISHERMAN'S WHARF. POSSIBLE 211 IN PROGRESS.

LET'S DO THIS.
NOT SO FAST. EVERYONE INVOLVED WITH YOU PEOPLE HAS ENDED UP IN JAIL. I WANT SOME ASSURANCE THAT WON'T BE ME.
I WANT TO TALK TO HIM.

THAT'S NOT PART OF THE DEAL.

IF I DON'T TALK TO HIM FACE TO FACE, *WE HAVE NO DEAL.*

SUIT YOURSELF.

PLEASE LET OUR LORD KNOW THAT HE WON'T DEAL UNLESS IT'S FACE TO FACE.
UNACCEPTABLE.

JUST LIKE I THOUGHT. EVERYTHING EVERYONE SAYS IS TRUE.

WHAT'S THE MATTER, COWARD?!
I KNOW YOU'RE HERE! YOU *TOO SCARED* TO FACE ME?!

HERE WE GO.
BE CAREFUL WHAT YOU ASK FOR.
VRMMMM

COME ON. GET OUT OF THE CAR. SHOW YOUR FACE.

SHOWTIME.

THWAK

KILL HER.
CHK

WHAMM

BWAK

NOAH, I GOT HER. ANY SIGN OF MY MOTHER?
NOT YET.

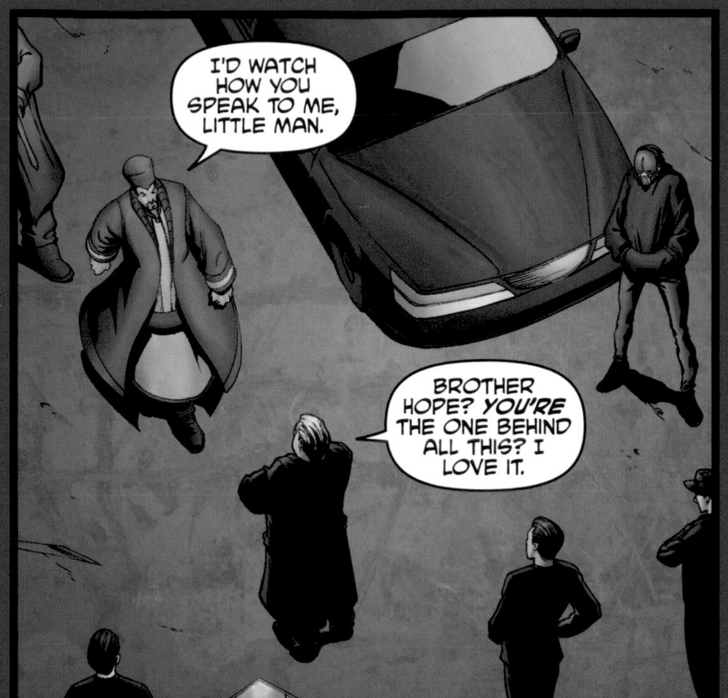
I'D WATCH HOW YOU SPEAK TO ME, LITTLE MAN.
BROTHER HOPE? YOU'RE THE ONE BEHIND ALL THIS? I LOVE IT.

DO YOU NOW?
SHOW IT TO ME.

SURE. YOU DON'T TRUST ME? I GUESS HOW COULD YOU, SINCE NOBODY CAN TRUST YOU. HA, HA.

YOU FIRST.

NEW AND CRISP. WHAT IS THIS, FROM YOUR SUNDAY DONATIONS? AHA, HA!

YOU'LL NEED THESE.

PSSSSH

NICE TRICK. YOU KNOW MONEY *SHOULD* GLOW.

I DON'T GET IT. WHY ARE YOU PAYING TOP DOLLAR FOR USELESS ARTIFACTS?
THAT IS NONE OF YOUR CONCERN.

YOU GOTTA TELL ME, MAN. YOU GOT SOME SORT OF ART FETISH? AS POPULAR AS YOU ARE, YOU COULD HAVE GOTTEN THE ITALIAN GOVERNMENT TO LET YOU HAVE IT. PRACTICALLY THE WHOLE WORLD BELIEVES YOU'RE A SAINT. IT'S THE *BEST COVER I'VE EVER SEEN.*

YOU MEAN *THE LAST.*

WHAT?

SHHKKK

BUDDA
BUDDA
BUDDA
NNF!
BUDDA
BUDDA

LET'S MOVE OUT. THE NIGHT IS YOUNG.
YES, MY LORD.

W-WAA?!
VWWOOOOM

BRAKOW

GO!

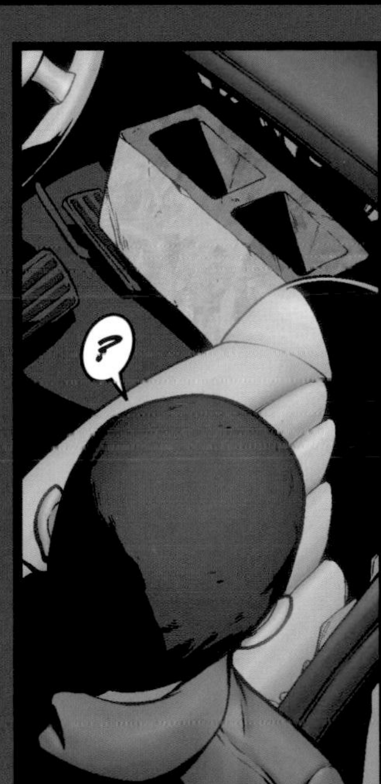
?

HELLO SIRACH.

I WONDERED WHO NOAH WAS WITH IN CENTRAL PARK. THE SACRED MOTHER HERSELF. IT'S BEEN A LONG TIME, MARIAH.
NOT LONG ENOUGH.

SUCH AN ANGRY TONE FOR AN OLD FRIEND. OH RIGHT, I KILLED THE GREAT CANDOR.
AND HE KILLED *YOU* FROM WHAT I GATHERED.

A MINOR SETBACK. I MUST SAY YOU'VE AGED WELL.
PROBABLY SHOULD HAVE LAID OFF THE DONUTS, BUT TIME HAS NOT *TOTALLY* BEEN YOUR ENEMY.

I'VE COME TO REASON WITH YOU.
SIRACH, YOU HAVE TO STOP.
YOU CAN'T REASON WITH A *MADMAN.* ISN'T THAT WHAT THEY CALLED ME?
HAVE YOU SEEN THE SHAPE THE WORLD IS IN?
DO YOU *REALLY* THINK I'M NOT NEEDED?

YOUR PLAN DIDN'T WORK *BEFORE* AND IT *WON'T WORK NOW.*

WHY? BECAUSE THE MANTAMAJI ARE GOING STOP ME AGAIN? REALITY CHECK. *THEY ARE ALL DEAD!*
WELL, EXCEPT FOR YOUR SON. WHERE IS THE SO-CALLED CHOSEN ONE?

THAT'S RIGHT, I *KNOW* MARIAH. WE ARE FOREVER LINKED, HE AND I, WHICH IS WHY THIS MEETING IS SO FITTING.
YOU WILL TELL ME WHERE THIS GREAT SAVIOR IS AND I WILL GIVE HIM A CHOICE, SURRENDER TO ME OR *WATCH HIS MOTHER DIE.*

YOU WILL *NEVER* FIND OUT.
FWSH
FWSH

DON'T THINK FOR A SECOND YOUR *PITIFUL* BIO BLASTS WILL HAVE ANY EFFECT ON ME.

HOW ABOUT MY SWORD.

NOAH! EXCELLENT. THIS IS TURNING INTO QUITE A REUNION.

LET HER GO SIRACH, OR--
OR WHAT? I'VE BEATEN YOU EVERY TIME WE'VE FACED EACH OTHER.

WELL TONIGHT HE HAS HELP.

THIS JUST KEEPS GETTING BETTER. THE SON, I PRESUME.
I'M DISAPPOINTED... USUALLY THE MANTAMAJI GET DRESSED UP TO DIE.

UNLESS IT'S BECAUSE YOU DON'T HAVE *A CLUE* AS TO WHAT THESE OLD FOOLS HAVE GOTTEN YOU INTO.
I KNOW I CAN'T DIE FROM SOMEONE TALKING ME TO DEATH.
FAIR ENOUGH.

NO!

ZASHHHH

BUDDA
BUDDA
BUDDA
BUDDA
BUDDA

BLAM
BLAM
tnk
tnk

CHOOOM

ZRSHH

SWAAAAASHH

SCHWAP

MARIAH, GET HIM OUT OF HERE!

COME ON NOAH. FOR OLD TIMES SAKE.
ZSHH

ZMMMMM

VWAAAASHH

OOF!
UNH!

BLAM
CHF
CHF
BLAM

WACK

ZWOOSH

THWAP

THWACK

OOMPF!

KTHUDD

ZWACK

WEEOO WEEEOO WEEOO
EHH. NOW IS NOT THE TIME.

KNIGHTS, *LET'S GO!*
LEAVE NO MAN ALIVE BEHIND.

HUH?

DOOSH

KRACK

RUN, GET AWAY, GET--

ACK

TAKE YOUR HANDS *OFF HER.*

KSHHK

I'M SORRY IT HAS TO BE THIS WAY, MARIAH, BUT KNOW YOUR DEATH IS SERVING A *BIGGER PURPOSE.*

MOM!!!

SLIIISSSH

CHAPTER 5

But even the Mantamaji were unsettled by death at times. In the heat of battle, honor and duty are boon companions, and danger seems a distant rumor; but when the fight is over, every dead body on a silent battle-field is a token of failure.

NO! NO!
NO!

HURRY UP. GET THEM IN THE TRUCKS. WE'RE LEAVING.

THUMP

HFF
HFF

HFF

BLAM
BLAM
BLAM
TNK
TNK

RIIIP

BLAM
BLAM

UNNH...

HN?!

OH NO,
NO.

ZZSH

QUASITANTI DES KAJOMBY.
HANG ON, MOM, *PLEASE.* HANG ON!

HEROES GIVE...SO OTHERS MAY LIVE. YOU ARE FREE.

GET UP!

COME ON, YOU KNOW THE RULES. NO KNIGHTS LEFT BEHIND ALIVE.

YOU GOTTA GET UP. I CAN'T CARRY YOU.

SORRY GUYS.
BLAM

?

WUDDA WUDDA WUDDA
WUDDA
WUDDA
WUDDA
WUDDA
WUDDA
WUDDA

ELIJAH?
ELIJAH?
ELIJAH?

MANHATTAN HOSPITAL
CAN YOU HEAR ME?

WHERE AM I?
MANHATTAN GENERAL.

MOM.

WHERE'S MY MOTHER? *WHERE IS SHE?*

MORGUE

HARLEM

ELIJAH, WHAT WERE YOU DOING DOWN THERE AT THE WHARF?
I TOLD YOU ALREADY.

NO. YOU ASKED ME TO NOT REPORT EVERYTHING AT THE HOSPITAL, WHICH I *DIDN'T.*
BUT WE'RE IN THIS TOGETHER NOW, SO YOU HAVE TO TELL ME *EXACTLY* WHAT WAS GOING ON TONIGHT.

I WAS WORRIED ABOUT YOU AND TRIED TO PROTECT YOU.

AND YOUR MOTHER CAME WITH YOU?

YES.

WHAT WERE YOU *THINKING?* I'M THE COP HERE. YOU'RE THE A.D.A. I DON'T NEED YOU AS MY GUARDIAN ANGEL.
DON'T YOU THINK *I KNOW THAT?!* I HAVE TO LIVE WITH THIS.

SO DO I! I'M SORRY. I NEVER SHOULD HAVE TOLD YOU WHAT WAS GOING ON.

IT'S NOT YOUR FAULT. IT'S MINE.
ALL I EVER WANTED WAS TO GET AHEAD AND MAKE MONEY.
IT'S BEEN MY SINGLE FOCUS FOR AS LONG AS I CAN REMEMBER.
WANTING A BETTER LIFE DIDN'T KILL YOUR MOTHER, ELIJAH. EVIL PEOPLE DID.

I JUST WISH I'D UNDERSTOOD WHAT SHE WAS TRYING TO SAY AND MAYBE I'D HAVE BEEN READY.

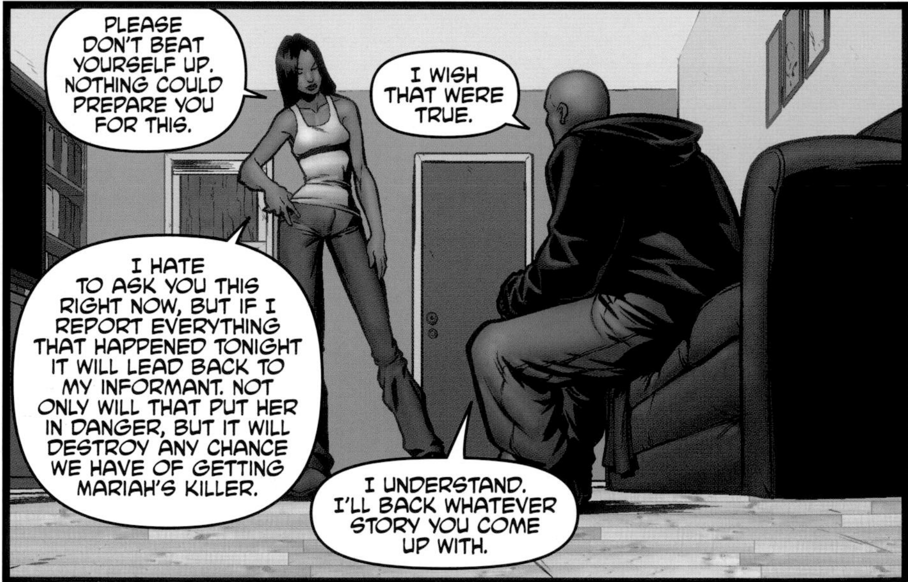
PLEASE DON'T BEAT YOURSELF UP. NOTHING COULD PREPARE YOU FOR THIS.
I WISH THAT WERE TRUE.
I HATE TO ASK YOU THIS RIGHT NOW, BUT IF I REPORT EVERYTHING THAT HAPPENED TONIGHT IT WILL LEAD BACK TO MY INFORMANT. NOT ONLY WILL THAT PUT HER IN DANGER, BUT IT WILL DESTROY ANY CHANCE WE HAVE OF GETTING MARIAH'S KILLER.
I UNDERSTAND. I'LL BACK WHATEVER STORY YOU COME UP WITH.

I PROMISE YOU, WE'LL FIND THE PERSON WHO KILLED YOUR MOTHER AND SEND THEM TO JAIL FOREVER.

I HAVE SOMETHING ELSE IN MIND.

WHAT DO YOU MEAN? WHERE ARE YOU GOING?
THIS IS MY FIGHT NOW. TIME TO TAKE FROM HIM WHAT HE TOOK FROM ME.

SO YOU KNOW WHO DID THIS?
DON'T WORRY ABOUT IT.
ELIJAH WAIT! IF YOU KNOW MORE THAN WHAT YOU'RE TELLING ME...

ELIJAH!
ELIJAH!

RING
RING

NOT A GOOD TIME.
WHAT HAPPENED TONIGHT?
I DON'T KNOW. I WAS KNOCKED UNCONSCIOUS.
SO THEY GOT WHAT THEY WERE AFTER?

IT WOULD APPEAR SO. WHAT WAS IT?
NOT SURE. KELLIS SAID WHAT THEY WERE GETTING FROM THE MOBSTER WAS SOMETHING THEY HAD TO HAVE. I'LL SEE IF I CAN GET BACK IN TOUCH WITH HER TO LEARN MORE.
KEEP ME POSTED.

ELIJAH!

HOPE'S TEMPLE

BLUE KNIGHT. YOUR SECT MAY REMOVE THEIR MASKS.

I AM NOT UNMINDFUL THAT SOME OF YOU HAVE COME FRESH FROM NARROW CELLS.

OTHERS BATTERED AND BEATEN WITH THE TRIALS AND TRIBULATIONS OF AN UNFORGIVING WORLD.

BUT THE BOUNTY FROM YOUR HARD WORK TONIGHT IS AS REAL AS THE HEART THAT BEATS INSIDE EACH AND EVERY ONE OF YOU.

YOU SEE. IT FEELS MY PRESENCE. IN THREE DAYS THE TOTEM WILL HELP ME GUIDE THE CRYSTAL TO CARRY OUT OUR MISSION.

BUT TONIGHT I WANT TO INTRODUCE YOU TO MY ETERNAL SPIRIT.
ZOOOSH

BEAUTIFUL, IS SHE NOT? THIS WAS MY WIFE.

LIKE ME, SHE HAD GROWN TIRED OF THE WAYS OF MAN AND BELIEVED IN A BETTER PATH.

BUT BECAUSE WE WERE TRYING TO CHANGE THIS WORLD, WE WERE MET WITH OPPOSITION.

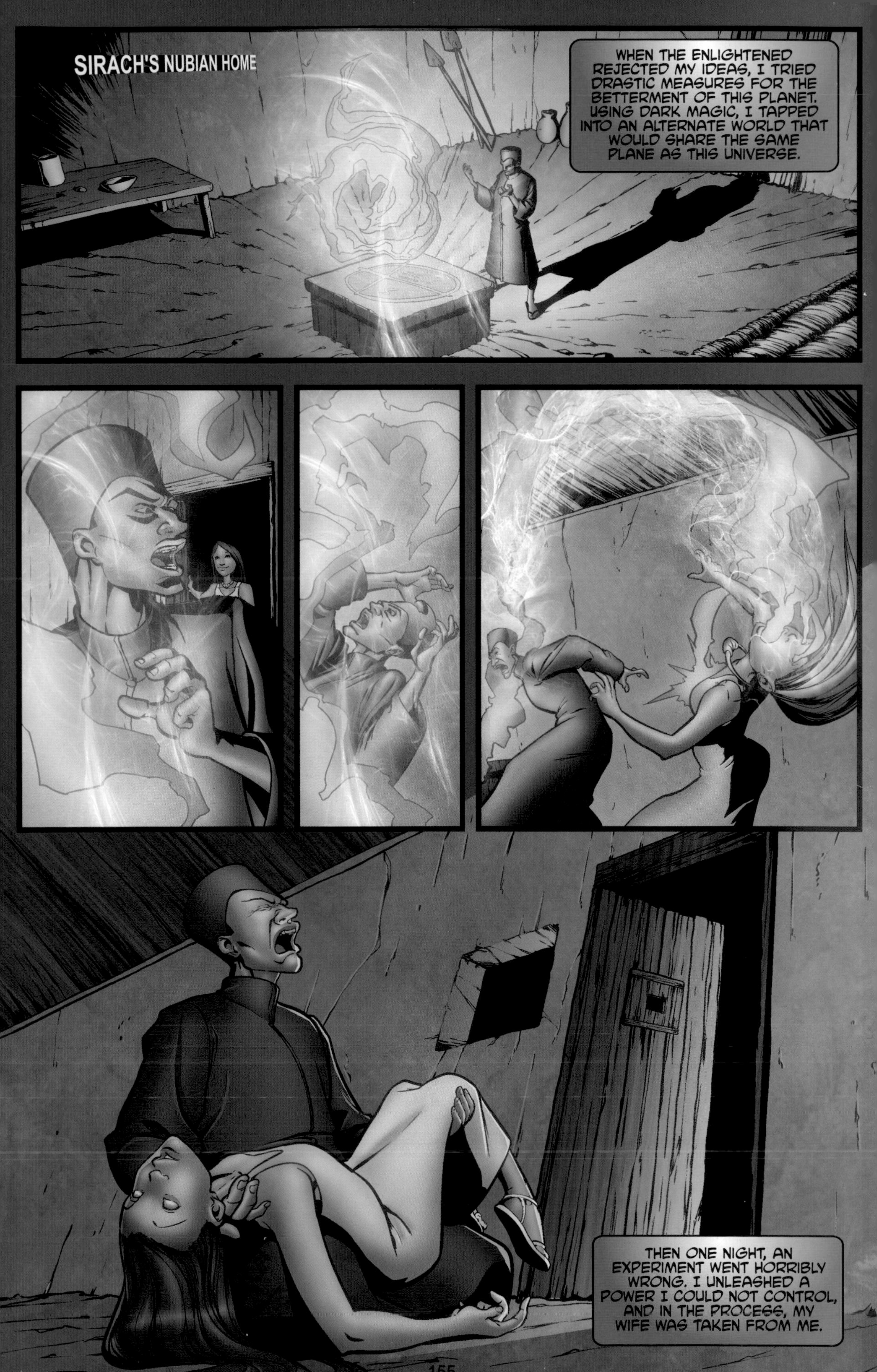
SIRACH'S NUBIAN HOME
WHEN THE ENLIGHTENED REJECTED MY IDEAS, I TRIED DRASTIC MEASURES FOR THE BETTERMENT OF THIS PLANET. USING DARK MAGIC, I TAPPED INTO AN ALTERNATE WORLD THAT WOULD SHARE THE SAME PLANE AS THIS UNIVERSE.
THEN ONE NIGHT, AN EXPERIMENT WENT HORRIBLY WRONG. I UNLEASHED A POWER I COULD NOT CONTROL, AND IN THE PROCESS, MY WIFE WAS TAKEN FROM ME.

I SOUGHT HELP FOR MY MISTAKE, BUT THEY ONLY WANTED ME TO STAND TRIAL AS AN EXAMPLE FOR OTHERS.

ONE OF THEIR LEADERS TRIED TO DEFEND ME.

BUT I KNEW THE ERROR OF THEIR WAYS AND WOULD NOT STAND IN SILENCE. I SPOKE MY MIND AND WAS CONDEMNED FOR IT.

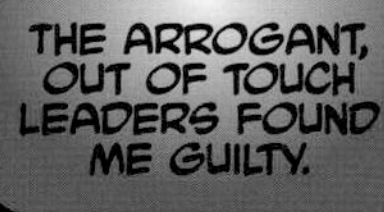
THE ARROGANT, OUT OF TOUCH LEADERS FOUND ME GUILTY.

MY OWN BROTHERS AND SISTERS BRANDED ME AN OUTCAST.

I WAS EXILED, BUT I KNEW WHAT I HAD TO DO.

BEYOND THE SAHARA, I FOUND A DOOR BETWEEN UNIVERSES, PULSING WITH DARK MAGIC.

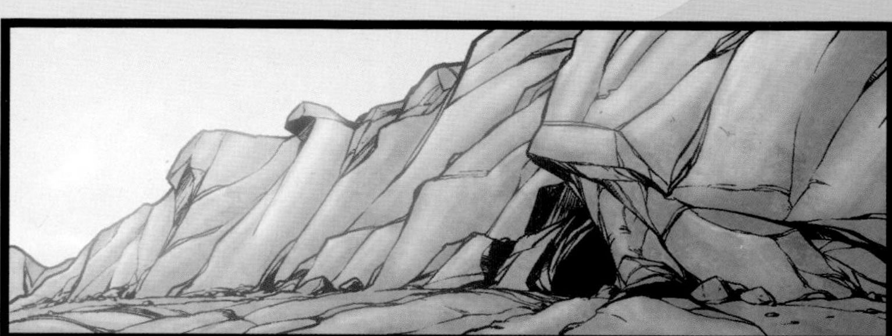

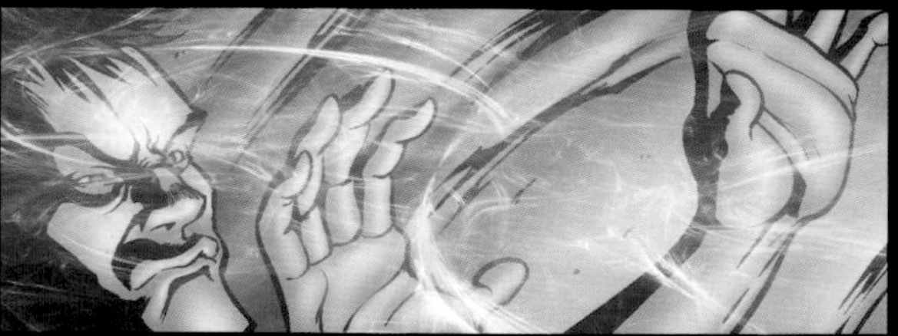

REALIZING I NOW HAD THE POWER TO REIGN OVER HUMANITY I RETURNED HOME.

TO LET MY OPPRESSORS KNOW WHAT BETRAYAL FELT LIKE.

THEY TRIED TO STOP ME, BUT THEIR POWER CAME FROM THIS UNIVERSE ALONE. I WAS FILLED WITH THE POWER OF TWO!

BUT EVEN THOUGH MY ACTIONS WERE JUSTIFIED, I WAS STILL COLD INSIDE.
SHWOOM

IT DIDN'T BRING MY WIFE BACK, AND I WAS STOPPED FROM OBTAINING MY GOAL--WHICH WAS ALWAYS TO MAKE CHANGE.
HSSSS

I WANT YOU TO UNDERSTAND, I'M NOT TRYING TO DESTROY THIS WORLD.
I'M TRYING TO CREATE A PERFECT ONE. A WORLD WHERE PEOPLE LIKE YOU CAN LIVE OUT YOUR DREAMS IN *PEACE.* IN *LOVE.*

BUT THERE ARE THOSE OUT THERE THAT WANT YOU TO REMAIN POOR AND BROKEN. THEY DON'T WANT YOU TO SUCCEED BECAUSE THEY KNOW FOLLOWING ME WILL MAKE YOU FEEL... WHAT, KELLIS?

SPECIAL?
EXACTLY!

LIKE INSECTS THEY INFEST OUR HOME AND TRY TO DESTROY IT...

FROM WITHIN. KELLIS, LET ME ASK YOU ONE MORE QUESTION.

WHEN DID THE BRAND OF SIRACH BECOME REMOVABLE?

SHE'S A SANCTUANT!
SHOOM

GET HER!

HYUNN!
DON'T LET HER OUT!

AAGH!
≠HFF≠
≠HFF≠
HOW COULD YOU, KELLIS?

!

WAIT! PLEASE STOP! YOU DON'T UNDERSTAND!
LET ME EXPLAIN.

HOW LONG DID YOU THINK YOU COULD HIDE FROM US?

I JUST WANTED TO FOLLOW YOUR WORD.

THEN WHY DIDN'T YOU REVEAL YOUR TRUE NATURE TO US?
I WAS AFRAID YOU WOULD NOT ACCEPT ME.

WHO ARE YOU WORKING FOR? POLICE, SANCTUANTS, OR BOTH?
NO. PLEASE, I BELIEVE IN YOU.

COMMIT YOUR SOUL AND I'LL LET YOU LIVE.

I COMMIT.
I COMMIT.

HKAK!

NOW SACRIFICE YOURSELF IN THE NAME OF HOPE.
KAFF KAFF

SHHH
WHAT? BUT, I SUBMITTED TO YOU.

TO BE ONE OF US YOU MUST BE WILLING TO DIE FOR OUR CAUSE.
PLEASE, NO. HAVE MERCY.

MERCY, SANCTUANT? IS SOMETHING WE WILL NEVER HAVE.

WAIT. MY HANDS. WHAT ARE YOU DOING?

PLEASE... STOP I... I...
FWOOSH

AIIEEEEEE!

LET THIS BE A LESSON TO ALL OF YOU. WHAT WE SEEK IS A GIFT THAT MANY DON'T WANT US TO HAVE.

PROTECT WHAT YOU HOLD MOST DEAR AND TOGETHER WE WILL RISE UP FROM THE ASHES. TOGETHER WE WILL FIND SALVATION *BY ANY MEANS NECESSARY!*

HOPE!
HOPE!
HOPE!
HOPE!

HOPE'S TEMPLE
HOPE!
HOPE!
HOPE!
ARE YOU GOING TO STORM IN THERE BY YOURSELF?
IF I HAVE TO.
DO YOU KNOW WHAT YOU WILL FACE?
I DON'T CARE.
THEN YOU WANT TO END UP LIKE YOUR MOTHER?

DON'T *EVER* SAY THAT TO ME AGAIN.

YOU'LL *DIE* IF YOU DON'T LEARN HOW TO CONTROL YOUR ANGER AND FULFILL YOUR DESTINY.

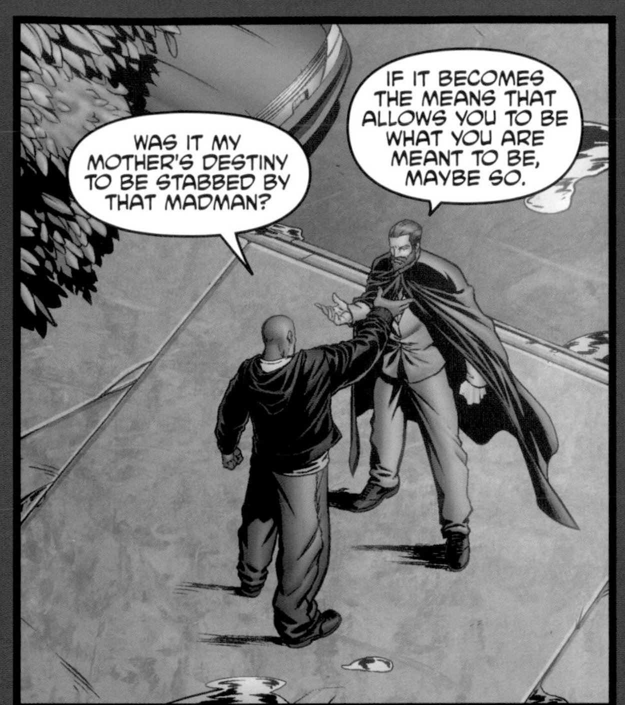
WAS IT MY MOTHER'S DESTINY TO BE STABBED BY THAT MADMAN?
IF IT BECOMES THE MEANS THAT ALLOWS YOU TO BE WHAT YOU ARE MEANT TO BE, MAYBE SO.

THAT'S NOT RIGHT.
THE *WORLD* IS NOT RIGHT. BUT YOU HAVE A GIFT THAT CAN FIX THAT.

THE CHOICE IS YOURS. WHAT SHALL IT BE?

LET'S GET ONE THING STRAIGHT, OLD MAN. WHAT HAPPENS TO THE WORLD IS NOT MY CONCERN. I'M GETTING REVENGE FOR MY MOTHER.

NOW SHOW ME WHAT I NEED TO KNOW.

TO BE CONTINUED

CHAPTER 6

It took the Mantamaji years to learn all the ways they could use their versatile weapons or to form shapes in men's minds. The Enlightened told them that long ago, the chosen warriors had even more powers—unlimited magical abilities; the stuff of legends. And who was to say that this legendary power might not return in the future? It was exciting to imagine, and a little terrifying.

ROOSEVELT ISLAND
TWO HOURS AGO

WHAT IS THIS PLACE?

HOME.

THE ABILITY TO CREATE ILLUSIONS.
DO YOU KNOW ANY FIGHTING TECHNIQUES?
ZWORP

KICK BOXING, TAEKWONDO. AS A KID MY MOM HAD ME IN EVERY STUDIO MARTIAL ARTS CLASS SHE COULD AFFORD.

SO YOU WOULD LEARN TO PROTECT YOURSELF WITHOUT TRIGGERING YOUR MAGIC. GOOD.
USE YOUR ANKH.

SHNNN

TO FIGHT LIKE A MANTAMAJI, YOU MUST LEARN HOW TO MOVE AND THINK LIKE ONE.

BWOOSH

HRNN!

NOT BAD, NOW FINISH ME OFF.

SWAP

DONE. WHAT'S NEXT?
hsssss

AS SOLDIERS, OUR POWERS MANIFEST THEMSELVES IN PHYSICAL COMBAT, BUT OUR MINDS CONTROL THE MAGIC.

BAP
BAP
BAP
BAP
BAP

SO IS THERE ANY "KRYPTONITE" THAT CAN MAKE US WEAK?

A GREEN ROCK THAT CAN... NEVER MIND.

WHAT CAN TAKE OUR POWERS OR KILL US?

IF WE LOSE CONCENTRATION, FOCUS, OR CONSCIOUSNESS, WE BECOME VULNERABLE. WE FEEL PAIN, GET SICK, DIE, EVERYTHING A HUMAN DOES, EXCEPT ONCE WE REACH ADULTHOOD THE AGING PROCESS SLOWS CONSIDERABLY.

HOW LONG *DO* WE LIVE?
NO ONE ACTUALLY KNOWS BECAUSE WE HAVE ALWAYS GIVEN UP OUR LIVES FOR HUMANITY.

CAN YOU BE ANY MORE DRAMATIC?

BOP
HEY!

PROTECT YOURSELF WITH YOUR ARMOR.

JUST AS YOUR MIND NATURALLY DID AT THE WHARF WHEN YOU WERE TRYING TO GET TO YOUR MOTHER.

SLRSH

THIS FEELS LIKE LEATHER AND METAL.
THAT'S BECAUSE IT IS.

AND HOW IS THAT SUPPOSED TO STOP BULLETS?
THE ARMOR IS AS STRONG AS YOUR MIND. IT ALL COMES DOWN TO FOCUS.

HEH.

UNNGH!

THWAKK

CONCENTRATE.

SLRSH

WOOOSH

THWOK

UNH!
TWAK

THWAP
GUH!

OKAY! OKAY! STOP! ENOUGH!

OW!

I THINK YOU FOUND YOUR GREEN ROCK.

JUSTICE CENTER
ONE HOUR AGO

WHAT HAPPENED?
THEY FOUND MY STREET INFORMANT, COMMANDER.
WHO ARE *THEY?* THE MAGICAL UNDERGROUND CRIME SYNDICATE YOU THINK IS BEHIND EVERYTHING?

THEY *ARE* OUT THERE SIR. THIS PRETTY MUCH PROVES IT.

ALL THIS *PROVES* IS THAT SOMEONE HAS THE *BALLS* TO DROP OFF A BURNT BODY IN FRONT OF MY POLICE STATION AND GET AWAY WITH IT. DON'T LIKE BEING THE JOKE HERE, SPENCER.
I KNOW SIR.
BEEP BEEP
SORRY, I HAVE TO TAKE THIS.

I'VE GOT BAD NEWS.
I CAN SEE THAT.

YOU'RE HERE. I'M SO SORRY.
THIS IS WHAT I GET FOR TELLING YOU I HAD A GIRL ON THE INSIDE.
ARE YOU SAYING THIS IS MY FAULT?'

WHY ELSE WOULD THEY LEAVE HER BODY ON YOUR DOORSTEP?
I DIDN'T BETRAY YOU. TELL ME WHERE HER KILLERS ARE AND I'LL PROVE IT TO YOU.
OH YOU WANT TO MARCH IN AND ARREST THEM?

ABSOLUTELY.
I'M PROTECTING MORE THAN JUST YOU HERE, SYDNEY. YOU SHOULD KNOW THAT BY NOW.
BUT I CAN'T DO MY JOB IF I'M TWO STEPS BEHIND.

I DON'T CARE ABOUT YOUR JOB. OUR LIVES DEPEND ON SOMETHING BIGGER THAN BOTH OF US.
THERE ARE ELEMENTS IN MOTION THAT YOU CAN'T SEE. AND UNTIL I GET A SIGN OF HOW THIS MIGHT ALL PLAY OUT KELLIS WAS THE BEST I COULD DO.

COULD?

WE'RE DONE. THIS WAS A MISTAKE AND KELLIS' DEATH IS ON BOTH OUR HANDS NOW.

CORNERSTONE? CORNERSTONE?

SPENCER! YOU DONE WITH THE PERSONAL CALLS? I HAVE SOME MORE QUESTIONS FOR YOU.

ZZZZZHH

SIRACH BELIEVED HE COULD ALTER THE COMPOSITION SO THE CRYSTAL WOULD NOT ONLY REMAIN OPEN, BUT *ENCOMPASS THE PLANET.*

ALLOWING HIM TO DO WHAT? I'M SURE NOT IMPROVE MASS TRANSPORTATION.
WE NEVER KNEW, JUST A PROMISE OF A NEW WORLD.
COULD HE BE SOMEHOW USING THE CRYSTAL WITH THAT MEDIA MERGER SATELLITE LINK HE SPOKE ABOUT IN CENTRAL PARK?
FOR SOMEONE WHO WANTS TO TAKE OVER THE WORLD I CAN'T IMAGE STARTING A LICENSE-FREE ALL WORLD TV CHANNEL IS OUT THE GOODNESS OF HIS HEART.
IF THAT IS THE CASE, WE HAVE FOUR DAYS TO STOP SIRACH FROM USING THE POWER OF THE CRYSTAL ON A GLOBAL SCALE.

SO WHAT'S THE PLAN?

SIRACH BUILT A COMMUNITY CENTER IN EACH OF THE FIVE BOROUGHS. THEY HAVE BECOME HIS STRONGHOLDS IN THE NEIGHBORHOODS.
OUR FIRST MOVE IS TO CRIPPLE HIS ARMY...

WHAT ARE YOU DOING?
YOUR MOTHER FREED YOUR POWERS BUT I'M GOING TO UNLOCK YOUR MIND TO GIVE YOU THE ABILITY TO DO MORE THAN CREATE STAFFS TO SPAR WITH.

I'LL KNOW HOW TO USE ANY WEAPON I THINK OF?
THIS MAY SEEM LIKE A SHORT CUT BUT I WON'T LIE TO YOU. ANYONE WHO HAS FACED SIRACH HAS DIED.

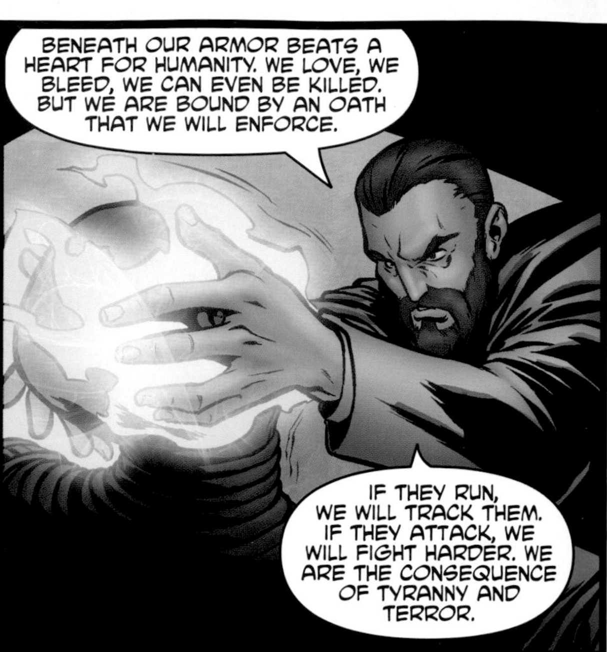

AS THE LAST TWO OF OUR RACE, WE REPRESENT OUR BROTHERS WHO LAID DOWN THEIR LIVES FOR ALL MANKIND. WE STAND UNITED PROTECTING THE INNOCENT FROM THE GUILTY, THE GOOD FROM THE EVIL.

WE WILL NOT REST UNTIL WE HAVE WON. WE ARE JUSTICE. WE ARE WARRIORS. WE ARE

MANTAMAJI.

AAAAAHHHH..!

COMMUNITY OUTREACH CENTER, TONIGHT

HOPE

HOPE COMMUNITY CENTER

SORRY WE'RE LATE. WE HAD TO TAKE CARE OF A TRAITOR.

I HEARD SHE WAS WITH YOU AT THE WHARF.

LET'S GET STARTED. WE HAVE TO HAVE ALL THE COMPUTERS AND WEAPONS LOGGED AND DISTRIBUTED IN FOUR DAYS.

KRKK

I'M SORRY, THAT DOOR SHOULD HAVE BEEN LOCKED. WE ARE CLOSED FOR THE EVENING.

YOU MEAN PERMANENTLY.
SLLSH

BAMF
HEY!

UWAAH!

KRSSHH

CHOK

ZZZT

CHAK

WHAT IN THE--

KONK

NNN...

WHAT HAPPENED TO THE LIGHTS?

WHO'S THERE?

THUDD

AH, WAIT, DON'T!
SOMEONE STOP...UGH!
LET ME GO!
OKAY.
There is no peace without Hope
There is no future without Hope

SHUMP

SKRSH

BAMF

WHAT ARE YOU SUPPOSED TO BE?
WE MET THE OTHER NIGHT AT THE WHARF.
SKI MASK? THE HELMET IS AN UPGRADE. SORRY ABOUT THE OLD LADY.
NO YOU'RE NOT AND IT MAKES WHAT I'M ABOUT TO DO ALL THE MORE SATISFYING.

YOU *REALLY* THINK YOU CAN TAKE *ALL TWENTY OF US* ON YOUR OWN?

I REALIZE IT'S NOT A FAIR FIGHT...

BADDA
BADDA

SLRSH
BLAM
BLAM

KRAAASH
BLAM
BLAM
BLAM
BLAM
SLRSH
SLRSH

AKKA
BRAKKA

SHH
BRAKKA
BRAKKA
KRSCHH
SHH

BLAM
BLAM
BRAKKA
BRAKKA
BRAKKA

HYUNH!

RAHH!

tnk
THOK

AAHH!

KLUNK

...FOR YOU.

WHAP

THIS IS FOR --

WAKOOOM

BOOOOOM

THWAK

KRUNCH
OOF!

WHY ARE THEY FIRING THE CANNONS? DO THEY WANT THE COPS DOWN HERE?
I'LL CHECK UP FRONT. I HAVE TO TAKE THIS TO THE BASEMENT.

HUH?

OOMF!

SHOOT HIM! SHOOT HIM!

BADDA
BADDA
BADDA

BADDA
BADDA
BADDA
SKRRRSH
HYAAA!

NOK

RARRGH!
WAK

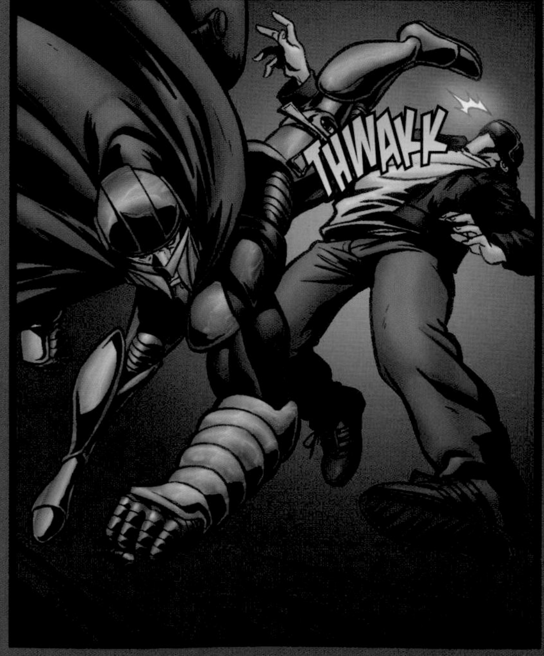
THWAKK

KYLAK

NICE SHOT.

HIS ARMOR IS COMING OFF.
HE WAS AT THE WHARF.
WHO IS THIS GUY?

PUT THE FIRE OUT BEFORE THIS WHOLE PLACE BLOWS UP, THEN DIG HIM OUT. I WANT TO TAKE HIS BODY TO SIRACH MYSELF.

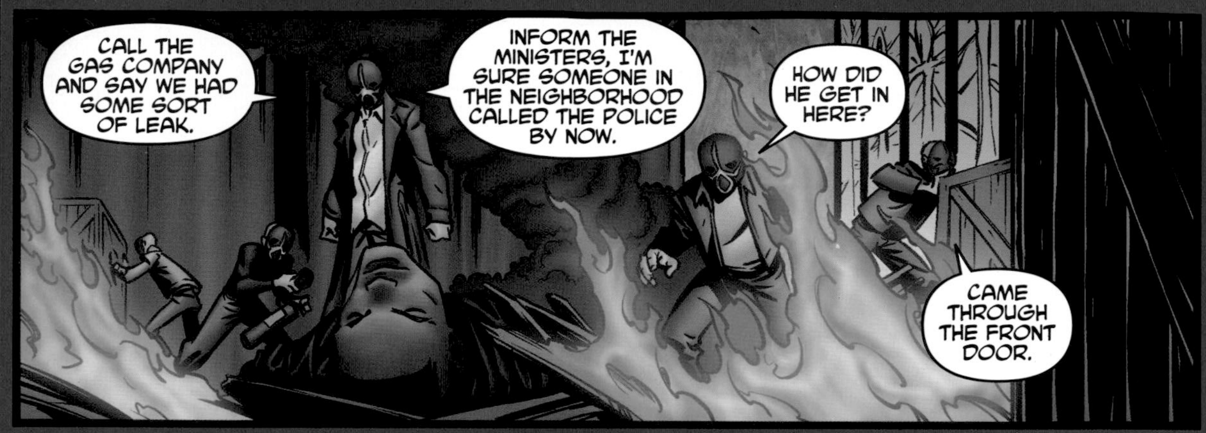
CALL THE GAS COMPANY AND SAY WE HAD SOME SORT OF LEAK.
INFORM THE MINISTERS, I'M SURE SOMEONE IN THE NEIGHBORHOOD CALLED THE POLICE BY NOW.
HOW DID HE GET IN HERE?
CAME THROUGH THE FRONT DOOR.

WHAT KIND OF SECURITY ARE YOU PEOPLE RUNNING DOWN HERE? WAS HE ALONE?
STILL CHECKING, SIR. KNIGHTS ARE DOWN ALL OVER THE PLACE.

HERE YOU GO, SIR.
IT'S LIGHTER THAN IT LOOKS.

BRING HIM OVER HERE.

LET'S SEE WHAT WE GOT?

YOU GOT TROUBLE.

SKRSSH

KONK

UGH!

TAT TAT TAT
TAT TAT
FALL BACK!
FALL BACK!
TAT
SHOOT HIM!
TAT TAT

GO! GO!
MOVE!

HUH?

BRAKKA BRAKKA
BRAKKA

HRRAARGH!

KRAK

TWOK

BAMF

KLAAAK

THWAK

KLUDD

CHOK

HELP... PLEASE...

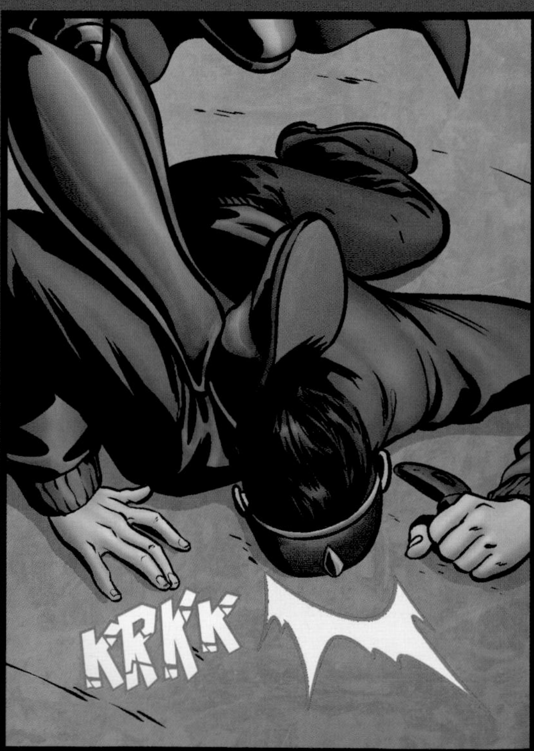
KRKK

CLOK

BRANDISH YOUR WEAPON!
ZZZSH

SSZZHH

KRUKK

KLONK

FWUP FWUP
FWUP FWUP

SWP

TWO STRAYS AT THREE O'CLOCK.

NICE.

NOT FOR LONG.

WE GOTTA GET TO A PHONE.

AHHHH!!

HELLO NOAH.

OH IT HURTS. I THINK MY LEG IS BROKE.

HERE'S SOMETHING FOR THE PAIN.

AND ON THAT FATEFUL NIGHT --

THEY STORMED THE VILLAGE AND LAID DOWN THE LAW THAT EVIL WOULD FALL.

WHO...ARE YOU?

I AM... A
MANTAMAJI

KRAAACK

TO BE CONTINUED

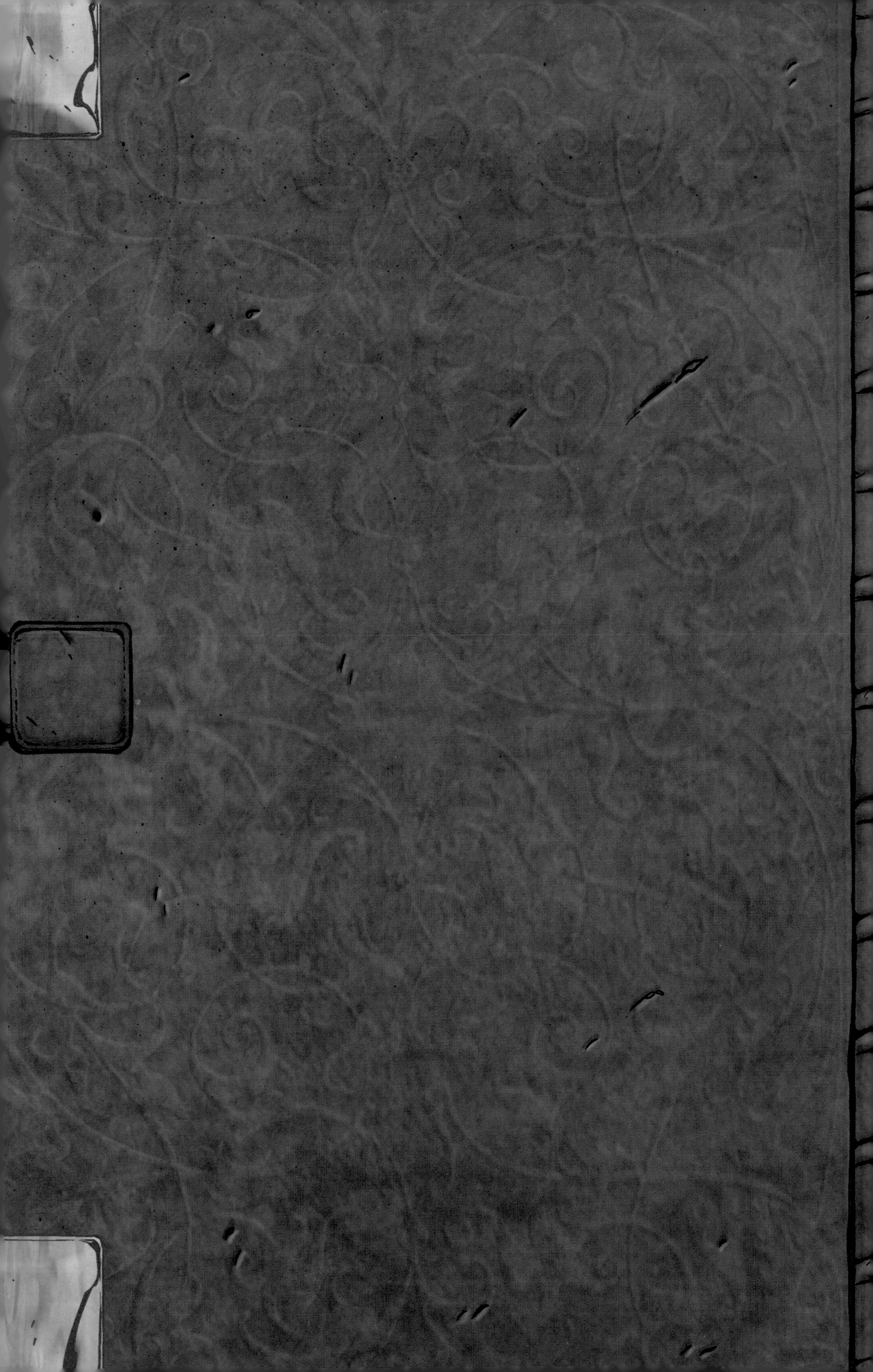

LEGEND OF THE MANTAMAJI: BOOK 2

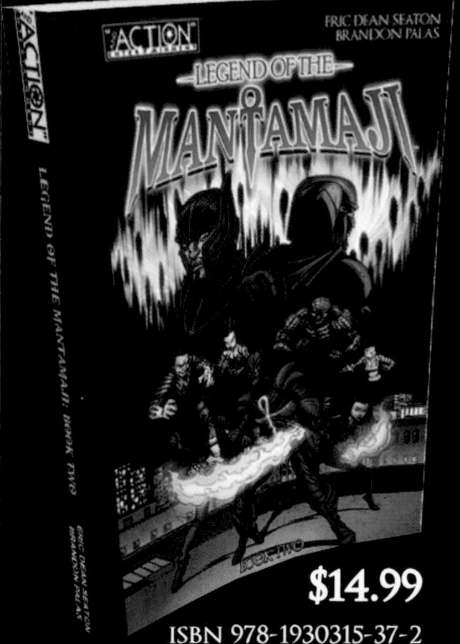

LEGEND OF THE MANTAMAJI

In a single week, Elijah Alexander has gone from being a famous and successful ADA in New York, to a hunted, haunted renegade on a mission of vengeance. Because Elijah is the last of a race of ancient warriors called the Mantamaji who once fought the world's greatest evils. And now the greatest evil of all has just reappeared and seeks to destroy the world as we know it. Elijah's the only one who knows how to stop this, and the only one with the power to get it done—because it takes a warrior to kill a mystical being. Or four of them.

ON SALE DECEMBER 10, 2014

$14.99

ISBN 978-1930315-37-2

STORY BY ERIC DEAN SEATON
FULL COLOR
184 PAGES

ART BY BRANDON PALAS
LETTERS BY DERON BENNETT
COLORS BY ANDREW DALHOUSE

WWW.LEGENDOFTHEMANTAMAJI.COM

Legend of the Mantamaji: Book 3